F*CK OFF CANCER

You've got this

xo

Linda

F*CK OFF CANCER

Cancer,
shaken,
not stirred,
on the rocks
with a twist!

LINDA BROSSI MURPHY

Published by Ingram Spark

Library of Congress Control Number: 2014919831

Hardcover: 978-0-9909216-7-7

Paperback: 978-0-9909216-0-8

EBook: 978-0-9909216-2-2

Top Notch Editing Team:

Victoria Wright, Victoria@bookmarkservices.net

David, Linda B, Sharon, Susan M, Adrianne, Claire and Susan E

Cover Design and Interior Layout by AuthorSupport.com

Dedication

This book is dedicated to my husband, David,

For finding my lump,

getting his Google MD for me,

not laughing at my gray Afro,

and sticking by my side through this unplanned detour.

~~~~~~~~~~~~~

This book is in loving memory of

my mother-in-law and friend

Elizabeth Metcalfe Murphy

Kind, thoughtful, and loving

June 1, 1932–April 5, 2014

Contents

CHAPTER 1

F**k Off, Cancer!

I am writing this book now because based purely on cold statistics, I only have a 68 percent chance of survival...The only time in my life I get a D on something, and it is the time that matters most. Sorry, already I digress.

It all began on October 2, 2012. My husband and I were having a weekday midmorning romp, a luxury a couple has when they both work from the house, all of the children are at school, and they are both awake. This particular morning, my husband was paying a lot of attention to "the girls," something I appreciate after nearly twenty-seven years of marriage.

His enthusiastic groping led to the discovery of a lump. "Hey, hon, this feels funny. I don't remember this before...." And so it began.

After I verified his discovery and we basked in postcoital bliss for a full thirty seconds, I rushed off to call my gynecologist, the other man in my life who pays close attention to the girls even though it is only once per year. My regular gyno was on vacation, so I took the open appointment for the afternoon and was being felt up by this covering doctor by two o'clock. He was not impressed at all with David's discovery. It didn't feel like much to him...I was not sure if I was relieved or insulted that my boobs were unimpressive. He prescribed a testosterone medication called Danazol and assured me that this mass, probably caused by some hormones, should shrink. He told me to return for a follow-up visit after my period.

I skipped out on my merry way. *Phew, I don't have cancer.* This older doctor with his experience and wisdom used his X-ray vision and gave me a clean bill of health. I made an appointment with my regular doctor for October 19 and filled my prescription on the ride home.

Over the next two and a half weeks, I cursed this doctor as I gained nine pounds, got a yeast infection and acne, and my voice started to crack. This medication was making me miserable, and during my daily breast exams, I assumed the lump was larger one day, next day smaller. Had it disappeared? I had no clue.

One of my sisters-in-law was visiting and was suspicious about my doctor's appointment, I came clean about the concern and she came along for moral support. Dr. Paul Dunn was back from vacation. I started the appointment by tossing the Danazol bottle at him and listing my complaints about this drug.

He looked at the ground and shook his head. "I never prescribe this medication for that exact reason." He proceeded to exam my lump. My boobies had never had so much attention. He wasn't impressed either, but as is customary when one finds a lump, he sent me for an ultrasound and mammogram. (Which of course I should have had two and a half weeks before.)

The appointment was scheduled for Halloween. I changed into my johnny and waited to bounce between mammogram and ultrasound at UMass Memorial Hospital in Worcester.

I didn't think I would ever get cancer. Let me rephrase that: I was 100 percent convinced every year when I had my mammogram that it would not find anything. I would *never* have breast cancer. Even sitting in the waiting room on Halloween, I felt the same way.

After all, let's look at the situation; my boobs have no meat in them. After nursing three children out of engorged D cups, I was left with globs of mashed potatoes the size of golf balls hanging in jock socks. Yes, they are respectable C cups, but that is only after I take the golf ball and roll it up into the PhD-engineered Victoria's Secret bra that can make even a pizza box look like it has breasts with the right style.

Even though I was so convinced I would never have cancer, did I skip mammograms? No, I went faithfully every year. Ironically, my last clean mammogram was last Valentine's Day, just seven and a half months prior to this fun. No clue what it is about me and mammograms on these just-for-fun holidays.

So off I went—mammogram—nothing exciting. Then I had the ultrasound. The technician, Erin, found the lump manually then used the wand and presto, saw the lump. She spent a lot of time measuring it and taking pictures. The last ultrasound I had was when I was pregnant, and I must say it was way more fun than this. Those pictures I couldn't wait to take home and show my friends...these, not so much.

During the ultrasound I got my first clue that, despite my unimpressed doctors, this was cancer. Erin's face was an open book. *I'm screwed!* She left the room in hopes of finding a doctor who could do a biopsy *stat*. I was very grateful for her *get-it-done* attitude since I was already twenty-nine days post-lump discovery. I was still aggravated about my two-and-a-half-week Danazol delay. No luck finding a doctor to do an ASAP biopsy, but now I knew this was serious.

Now, back to mammography to try and find this elusive lump using magnification. Voilà, we could see a little speck or two of calcification. How did I know this? Because I am the person who leaps out of the machine as soon it unclamps me to see the pictures. I never have a clue what I am looking for, and the technician usually gets annoyed, but it is my boob after all. I should be able to check out its innards when I get the chance.

After I was dressed, Erin took me aside into a little room. With the widest smile she could muster and a positive attitude, she encouraged me to make an appointment with a surgeon "just in case" my biopsy, which was scheduled for the following week, came back as cancerous. After all, she told me, it would be easier to cancel it when everything was fine than to have to wait longer to make it if the results warranted it. So it was this exact moment when I knew I had cancer. Although Erin tried to tell me this is her standard recommendation, I could tell she had seen thousands of ultrasounds and biopsies; she knew what she was talking about.

OMG, I have cancer!

Now that I knew, unofficially, that I had cancer I was in action mode. I asked for a copy of my films from today because, coincidentally, my daughter was dating the son of a radiologist who reads these films all day long. Marylou, Justine's boyfriend's mother, swung by my house on her way home from work that night. We lied to my daughter that the visit was about joining me, my mother-in-law, Betty, and my father's girlfriend, Marilyn, for a Caribbean cruise with the Irish Stars, which until this afternoon, I was sure I was going on in February. This was actually my life: I was planning on sharing a room with these two amazing senior citizen ladies, both of whom I adore, and listening to Irish singing—all week long.

My daughter was mortified that Marylou would even consider joining us on this adventure. We kept up the façade. I was unable to open the films at my house because I don't have the funky program I needed, but I sent her away with them and knew that they were in good hands.

Marylou conferred with her friend Susan, who happened to be a radiologist at Memorial. Susan would do my biopsy on Monday. More waiting.

As I mentioned, I am a woman of action. I was now operating as a woman who has cancer. I texted my cancer survivors, Tammy, Marilyn, and Heidi, on the pretext that one of the

Assumption girls, the friends I am still close to from my days at Assumption College, had cancer. Who was their doctor?

I then proceeded to call UMass Worcester, the Brigham-Faulkner Breast Center, and Massachusetts General Hospital. I made appointments for the week of November 15. Because this was all new to me, I didn't even know which type of doctor I needed. So to start, I needed a surgeon. I thought you needed an oncologist first, but that actually isn't until much later in the process.

Next, I had to figure out the cruise situation which became nonrefundable after November 1—today. Because I am an idiot, I didn't buy insurance. Who books a cruise with an eighty-year-old without getting the insurance? Ironically, though, I was the one with the medical issue.

The cruise people were amazing. They agreed, and confirmed via e-mail, that I could extend my 100 percent refundable period until November ninth, after I got my biopsy results. By then I would know for sure whether or not this was the big C and could cancel if I needed to. If it was not cancer I would definitely buy insurance in case anything else came up.

During the weekend I visited with lots of family. On November 2, my husband's birthday, we were actually with my in-laws in North Carolina and I did not breathe a word about the situation. A couple of friends knew about David finding the lump but until the doctor told me the facts, I saw no need to have too many people aboard this emotional, arduous roller coaster.

My husband, David, drove me to the biopsy on Monday morning. The emotions were getting the best of me, and I was all welled up and scared about the biopsy. I asked him to stay with me while I waited for the doctor. He was totally there for me; then he got kicked out so they could do the biopsy.

Having a personal connection to Dr. Susan really made a difference. Susan and I talked about my daughter and the Facebook prom pictures she had seen and other little items, which helped calm me down. At first I was watching the ultrasound screen that she was using to guide her, but I was sure that this was going to lead to me fainting, so I looked away. Before turning away I got to see an enormous needle, used to numb the area, snaking through in my breast toward the lump. It totally grossed me out.

When Susan finished, she had three or four samples of the lump and a needle aspiration of an enlarged lymph node. They put a rush on the results and we were hoping to have them by Wednesday. I asked that the results be sent to my gynecologist, because I like him and know him and I thought he'd be able to tell me over the phone what I already was pretty sure of.

Yes...More waiting.

On Tuesday night, David, our friend John, and I headed to Boston for what we were hoping would be the victory party for Senator Scott Brown. We had never been very politically involved, but Scott Brown is such a stand-up person that we wanted to stand behind him, and we got a little involved in his campaign. We arrived at the party and it was filled with people, food, and drink. There was a band playing some great music, and the crowd was really dancing. Because I never let anything slow me down, I was boogying all night long. The only issue that I ran into was that the crowd seemed to have some BO problems going on. I'd be dancing for a while, grooving to the tunes, and I would be overwhelmed by somebody's BO. Not quite able to find the source, we moved to a different area and, lo and behold, more body odor. Apparently this group of Scott Brown supporters did not know how to shower properly.

One of the things we were looking forward to was to hear his daughter, Ayla Brown, who had been an American Idol contestant, perform. She came out and sang a few songs and really was quite good. Unfortunately, the night dragged on and on, while we waited for the election results. Eventually we found out that Scott Brown was not going to continue to be our senator.

So, at the end of the evening, John, David, and I loaded back into the car for our sad drive home, and it was at that point when I was overwhelmed by the smell of body odor once again. I realized it was me. I was the stinky dancer on the floor all night long, probably offending everyone I was near as I boogied on down with my arms flailing high in the air. Funny that because I had the sentinel node biopsy and couldn't wear deodorant, I already had things in my life that were different than they would be. Prior to my biopsy, I would never have gone out without deodorant and offended people. Just one of the many ways that my life was changing.

Wednesday morning, I called my gyno's office and asked them to call my cell phone as soon as they had the results. I did not want to come in, I just wanted the results.

Just before noon, I was sitting in the parking lot at the Framingham post office, and Dr. Dunn called. I knew that it was against all doctor etiquette to tell someone they have cancer over the phone, but I insisted. He confirmed...yes, it was cancer, but the good news was that it's *the good kind*, which can be easily treated. (He was talking about it being ER/PR positive, but we will deal with that later) He actually called to make an appointment for me at Umass Memorial before he called me, so I would have a next step, but he found out I already had made an appointment.

I thanked him for the call and told him I would be fine. I walked into the post office and mailed my package. Then on my way to visit a friend and her mom at the local nursing home, I called my husband and told him what we already knew. Life had dealt us a lump in the road.

CHAPTER 2

It's Official, It's Cancer

Now we needed to tell our nearest and dearest.
UGH! This, we were dreading. This list of VIPs was
my dad and Marilyn, my brothers, my in-laws, and
our three children. I called and told dad and Marilyn
I was coming over for dinner and bringing pizza.
After that I invited my brothers to my dad's house
for dinner. One brother said he had plans. I told him
it was mandatory, and being the great brothers they
are, they both said, "Okay, I will be there."

That afternoon, my husband and I drove to Bentley University to tell our son Doug. It would have been awkward with his roommates, so we dropped the bomb on him in the common room of his dorm. One thing was blatantly clear; it sucks to tell people you love that you are sick. To make it even more difficult, his roommate's mother, whom I really liked very much, was visiting her son and stayed around so she could visit with us, which I was clearly not in the mood for. I did stop up at the room after dropping the sad news on Doug and said hello. When she later learned of the true reason for the visit, she understood the situation and went out of her way to support Doug.

I could handle having cancer. It sucked, and I had a long road ahead of me. It was going to be long and painful, and I could die. I was actually fine with all of that. The part I could not handle was the pain on the faces of people I love. Making people I love and who love me sad was the hands-down worst part of cancer for me.

When we went to Dad's for dinner, and I told this group of people, who love me unconditionally, about my diagnosis, you could see their hearts breaking for me and the road ahead. When I saw the moment it passed through their minds that I had an illness that could kill me, that I might die before my time, that I might be the first of this group to go…it made me cry, not for me but for the pain my passing would cause them.

Three more *announcements* to go, and the VIPs would be done. Next, I Skyped my in-laws in North Carolina. Obviously, if I could handle an Irish Singers cruise for a week, sharing a room with my mother-in-law, Betty, we had a great relationship. For twenty-eight years, I have adored my in-laws, and telling them was almost as hard as telling my dad. With both of my in-laws on Skype, I told them the news and once again saw that I have caused others pain. Again, this was the worst part. We ended the call with my reassurance that it was a small lump, it was early, it was a "good kind," and I would be just fine.

Then I Skyped my son David Jr. He had been at the University of Richmond for over three years, and I had never Skyped him before, but I told him I needed to show him a new trick the dog did. He placated me by setting up Skype for this momentous occasion. For some reason, telling him was very tough. Maybe because he's the only one of my kids I couldn't hug after telling them something so sucky. Having to share this news, over and over again was awful!

Last but not least was my daughter, Justine, a senior in high school. Telling her wasn't as hard as I thought it would be. I think she was so relieved that her boyfriend's mother, Marylou, wasn't really considering going on the cruise with us, the fact I had cancer was manageable. We cried a tiny bit, but at that point, even I thought this would be a walk in the park, so we didn't dwell too much on the worst-case scenario.

Cancer to me was survivable. I did not know personally anyone who died from breast cancer. My sister-in-law, Tammy had it twice and made it look easy, although her mother died in her thirties from breast cancer. Heidi M., my friend from town, had a mastectomy on one side and a free tummy tuck, and it was a done deal. Sharon had a double mastectomy, and the doctor gave her a great new set of ta-tas. Marilyn had a lumpectomy and radiation, and aside from not liking the side effects of tamoxifen, she seemed no worse for the wear.

Yes, hearing the words that you have cancer is a punch in the gut. People die from cancer all the time. That's very scary, but many, many people survive. And as we all know but ignore, many more people die from heart disease—the boobs just have better press agents!

So I told the VIPs, cancelled the cruise by e-mailing my biopsy results to them, and then had to wait until the next week to take a tour of my cancer options.

I was hoping that the doctors would tell me I would get my best-case scenario: free boob job, free tummy tuck, keep my hair. That crossed two of my body-image problems off my list and cured me of cancer at the same time.

It is much easier to justify these vain cosmetic surgeries when they are done to save your life. Not to mention, they would be paid for by insurance—a win-win! I was actually thinking that if we got this surgery done soon enough, I'd try and get us back on the cruise and look amazing in a bikini to boot. How naïve of me.

Over the course of the next few days, I told a few friends who told a few friends and so on. Now almost everyone in my personal universe knew my plight. I was trying to keep it out of my work world, although I work for a small family property management business so most of my coworkers are family.

CHAPTER 3

Over the River and Through the Woods to the Doctors We Go…

First up was Dr. Robert Quinlan at UMass Medical Breast Center. It was absolutely the best place to start. This man is amazing. David and I arrived on time for our five o'clock appointment and behind me was a frantic woman who had just arrived for her four fifteen appointment. She got lost, she was totally stressed out, and she was by herself.

The sweet side of me had compassion…the other side of me thought that now the doctor will be running late, which he was, through no fault of his own.

At six fifteen we were finally escorted in to see Dr. Quinlan, an older dignified gentleman who arrived with a couple of sheets of paper and a box of magic markers. He just oozed compassion and understanding for my situation. He laid all the facts on the table by reviewing my biopsy results, highlighting phrases, drawing a tree of options, and explaining the road I was on and what lay ahead.

The news wasn't what I had hoped. My dreams of perky boobs and keeping my hair were shattered. We were talking lumpectomy, chemotherapy, radiation, and a year of a fairly new life-saving drug called Herceptin, which he explained was developed ten years ago by Dennis Slamon, MD, the chief of Hematology-Oncology at UCLA. Dr. Quinlan said if it wasn't for this man I'd be a goner (not quite in those words).

This was all because of the little acronym HER2+. Although I refused to actually understand it, if you want to learn about it, you need to read one of the million other things written on breast cancer. It was very aggressive and bad news for my hair follicles, but I needed mandatory chemo and Herceptin if I wanted to try to live. Okay, this sucked.

Dr. Quinlan's thorough explanation of my situation along with drawings was excellent. I left with highlighted papers in hand, knowing exactly what I was facing. I could head to my next two appointments with more confidence. I also felt that if the other appointments didn't go so well, I would be in good hands with this wonderful man. I left with an appointment for the following week with the cancer team to get the ball rolling.

This appointment revved up my husband. He came home and proceeded to read everything in sight (and by sight, I mean the entire Internet). Overnight, he was becoming a breast cancer expert. My friend Adrianne said my husband got his GD (Google doctorate) on the subject. He kept trying to get me on board by forwarding to me all the clearest articles and medical updates on HER2+. All of which I ignored.

I was entering *ostrich mode*. Head firmly in the sand. Here's my body; fix it. I will do exactly as I am told (although I will *not* remove my sculptured nails, my one act of rebellion) just do what you have to do!

Aside from the HER2+ bad news, the good news was that my tumor was ER/PR positive. This meant it was estrogen and progesterone receptor positive, or something like that, and for some reason this was a good thing because it would help the chemo do its job better. If you actually want to understand, you need to look elsewhere (my husband can send you some articles), because as I said, I was only along for the ride.

As I was traveling down this unanticipated path, I realized that although I had cancer, I was very, very lucky. I had a loving husband, wonderful supportive friends and family, a dependable car to get me around to all of these appointments, children old enough to take me to chemo, great health insurance, and a flexible job in a family business. If I could save a single mom with young children and no health insurance or support from having this disease by my getting cancer instead of her, I'd take one for the team. I could only hope that it worked that way.

Next up, we visited the Brigham and Women's Faulkner Hospital Breast Center. Both Tammy and Marilyn recommended this surgeon. Occasionally, there is a situation that seems to go wrong from beginning to end. Well, that's how it went at Brigham Faulkner. We were told to show up early to fill out paper work, but they didn't need any done. The waiting room had a big plate-glass window that was fogged up so you couldn't see out clearly. There were dead bugs on the windowsill and along the edge of the carpet and a cobweb string from the windowsill to my seat—yuck!

Our ten o'clock appointment time passed. A receptionist came over to us at 10:20 and told us that the doctor was here but having trouble parking and would be up shortly. That was actually a mistake. We always assume if a doctor is running late that they are saving a life—not that the line at Dunkin Donuts was longer than anticipated, and now they are late for our appointment. So we stayed in the gross waiting room a little longer, honestly already turned off by the experience prior to meeting the surgeon.

The surgeon then had difficulty with her computer and was unable to access the ultrasound that I brought. She did an exam, explained that a lumpectomy was best, and briefly mentioned that the HER2+ complicated things so I would need chemo. David and I exited as soon as we could. This wasn't the place for us.

Next on the docket was Massachusetts General Hospital in Boston. I had an appointment with Dr. Barbara Smith. A very odd coincidence connected the two of us. Dr. Smith's sister was my brother's next-door neighbor, and when they were between homes, she and her husband lived in his basement apartment. They are good friends. So my brother helped Dr. Smith's sister, and here she was helping me. It really is a small world!

The Mass General Yawkey Breast Center is a factory—actually a well-oiled machine. I already mentioned that I am vain, so the first thing I noted upon arrival was that next to the cancer center there was a boutique that sold wigs, scarves, jewelry, etc. I was so relieved by this that I almost booked the surgery before meeting Dr. Smith.

My husband and I were ushered to a room and settled in for what we were told would be a long afternoon. The radiation department came in first and explained all about radiation, which would happen because I was to have a lumpectomy, not a mastectomy. This was so far down the line, and we were already on data overload, that it was more of a blur. The only real info that grabbed my attention was that radiation on the left side requires a little more precision so they don't accidentally fry your heart. The chemos that I would be getting could already do a number on my ticker. Oh goodie, that sounded like fun.

When I met Dr. Smith, I liked her right away. She was elegant and poised, and I could just tell, smart as a whip. She also recommended a lumpectomy. So that ended my hopes and dreams of the tummy tuck and perky size Cs on the insurance company's tab. So three doctors out of three agreed, lumpectomy, which on the brighter side indicated that a lumpectomy was the correct procedure and a mastectomy would be overkill (no pun intended).

It was already November 15, forty-five days since the lump was discovered. I was feeling very impatient to get things moving. In the spring I had a double graduation coming up. On May 12, David Jr would graduate from the University of Richmond, and on June 7, Justine would graduate from high school. I was trying to figure out how fast I could plow through this mess, so I could feel good for these events. The sooner I started, the sooner I'd be done.

One thought that crossed my mind was, if the mammogram hadn't seen this lump in my left side, how did I know that there was no cancer in my right breast? Apparently Dr. Quinlan thought the same thing and had already scheduled an MRI for me in Worcester for the following week. Oddly, Dr. Smith and Dr. Quinlan both thought that the MRI was a good idea, but the surgeon that we saw at the Brigham was against an MRI, because she felt that frequently the results were false positive, causing needless angst and biopsies.

Although I still had to decide between Dr. Smith and Dr. Quinlan, I have preop blood work and a chest X-ray at Mass General, knowing the results could be used at either place after we decided which route to go.

On the ride home from Mass General, my husband and I discussed our options. He was voting for UMass for the ease of access of Worcester from our home, and he really liked Dr. Quinlan. I was leaning toward Mass General. People come from around the world to get the best care there. It didn't make sense not to go there just because it was a forty-five-minute ride; we would have to deal with that inconvenience. I didn't even know at the time that Mass General was voted the number-one hospital in the United States, pushing Johns Hopkins off their pedestal after a nineteen-year run.

After quite a few heated discussions, which were way more intense due to the stress of the situation, my husband ultimately said it was my decision, and I opted for Dr. Smith and the Mass General team. Yes, it was going to take an already time-consuming situation and make it more time-consuming, but getting the best care was worth it. At Mass General, I was not their first rodeo. They'd *been there and done that* thousands of times over. I was hoping that making me a survivor was second nature.

On Monday, November 19, I had my MRI in Worcester. In this crazy machine, your boobies just dangle in a couple of holes, and you need to lie 100 percent still for what seems like forever. I was initially afraid they might hit the floor, but the machine seemed to accommodate the droopy older boobies. I wished my college roommate and dear friend Michelle and I had entered the wet T-shirt contest during Fort Lauderdale college spring break, back when I had something to show.

When the MRI was done, yes, you guessed it: now I had to

wait for the results. I was thinking that there would be no issue, of course, because even after all this, I am, in fact, an optimist.

The day before my surgery, the surgeon called and said there was something suspicious on the MRI in the same breast. The right breast was free and clear. Well at least *righty* hadn't let in any intruders.

This meant the chance to get this lump cut out of me was now further delayed. Let's get the cancer out already! It also meant I might need a mastectomy if this is serious, which meant we couldn't schedule another surgery until we determined whether it was more cancer and would require more surgery. On the brighter side, although it might have been more surgery, it could mean a free boob job. A silver lining. But to be totally honest; I was losing my enthusiasm for this, and just getting a lumpectomy and keeping my saggy boobs almost seemed appealing.

This was a seemingly never-ending cycle of waiting.

During the course of conversation, as part of their diagnostic tools, they ask about every aspect of your body and if there are any other areas of concern. My right hip had been bothering me for about three months. It was so painful that after a period of walking, especially on a hard surface, I got to the point where I was limping. If I was getting into the passenger side of the car, I needed to lift my right leg with my hands to get it in the door.

Because I was now dealing with cancer, I decided that my hip would need to be put on the back burner. As it turned out, once you're on the oncology floor, nothing was as simple as an ache or pain anymore. They sent me for a bone scan on November 24 to be sure that whatever my hip problem was, it was not actually cancer that had metastasized to the bones.

I was injected with some type of radioactive dye and put onto a table where a machine would pass over my body and take a look at my bones. After my head had popped out from underneath the machine, I could see a screen with the results of the radiation deposits in my skeletal figure. My shoulders, elbows, hips, knees, and ankles all lit up due to some arthritis. More information than I wanted to know. As I watched the test, I noticed that my pelvic area was glowing very brightly, and I self-diagnosed an issue with pelvic or uterine cancer. There was a technician in the room with me, and I casually asked what the bright pelvic area represented. I was exceptionally relieved when he explained that it was my bladder full of the radiation that had already been processed through my body. Whew, that was a close one. The good news was that there did not appear to be any cancer in my bones. As I was leaving, I was given an informational card indicating that I was filled with nuclear waste, and I might set off an alarm if I went through some sort of security checkpoint over the next few days. Good to know.

On Wednesday, November 28, I had a 3-D mammogram and an ultrasound to find the new *area of suspicion*. They weren't able to figure out what we were looking for, so this led to a biopsy under MRI. I couldn't even imagine how they'd come up with so many unique ways to torture these poor boobies!

Luckily, the MRI biopsy was scheduled for Friday November 30, so I didn't have to wait too long. The exceedingly nice nurse practitioner admitted, "It should be hell!" It was expected to be so much so, they recommended a muscle/brain relaxant to help me get through it.

On Friday morning, we headed into Boston for an early morning appointment. I had taken the first-ever Ativan of my life and was feeling a little more ditzy than normal. They started an IV, and I had a team of people ready to get the show on the road. I was impressed by what a *me*-centered production this procedure was, probably because I was not fully aware of what was involved.

They positioned me in the MRI machine and wedged my left breast in a hole that on the previous MRI was just a dangle hole, and strapped me to the table literally from head to toe—I'm talking straightjacket-type strapping. They gave me a freak out button to press in case I freaked out, but honestly, I was already freaked out!

They inserted me into the tube, and the sounds began... Bang, bang, grind, bang, pop...They injected the magic dye, and there was more banging and popping. Then they told me they were beginning the biopsy. I thought they'd numbed the area, because I had no pain—just mental anxiety. They slid me out and inserted the instruments to extract a sample of the area of concern. Then they slid me back in to see if they were in the correct place. No such luck! Out I came. They readjusted the instruments and slid me back in for another look.

The nurse practitioner who'd set me up for this appointment was there as my cheerleader. In order to get this done, you need someone to tell you are doing a good job lying still and explain what is happening next.

Finally the instruments were in the correct place. They collected a sample, and I was released from my confines. This had been a miserable experience. I spent the afternoon in a business meeting, but I sat there having PTSD from the morning's procedures.

More waiting.

Another week passed, and the results showed that with all of the data and slides, it was just a funny thing, not cancer.

Back to a lumpectomy, now scheduled for December 11, two months and nine days post-lump discovery. This cancer thing was taking forever.

The day before surgery, I headed over to the mall to my favorite nail person, Kevin, to get my nails filled and have him remove one of my acrylic overlays so that during the surgery they could monitor my blood oxygen level through my fingernail. I had previously explained to Kevin that he had to be hyper-vigilant about cleanliness and sanitation with regard to working on my fingernails. There was a huge danger of infection for me when I started chemotherapy. Because of this, everything was sanitized twice before use, and items that weren't normally sanitized, like a nail file, were replaced with new ones each visit, to be sure they were germ-free.

When I was down to nine perfect nails and one ugly, stubby index finger, I headed out to my car. This was the first time that I broke down and cried. I realized that cancer was going to be a series of losses in my life; my fingernail was just the beginning. It was only the removal of my fingernail, but it was also the fact that I would no longer have control over every aspect of my life. I would have to make choices and do some things differently in order to get better, even though they'd be unpleasant.

The morning of my surgery, I did my regular workout—one

hour on the treadmill at four miles per hour and some abs and arms work. I am trying hard to age somewhat gracefully without my arm flab waving back at me too much. I was always looking for an excuse to avoid exercise, and I realized that this road I was on would give me the perfect excuse to avoid exercise. In reality, I do need to exercise to try and grow older—which I hope is still an option—gracefully.

I arrived for an afternoon surgery, our favorite time, because we avoided rush-hour traffic into Boston. I brought an entourage: my father, his girlfriend, Marilyn, my daughter, Justine, and my husband, David. I also brought my favorite gift so far, a blanket with a picture of my family on it, from friends, John and Susan, to snuggle in after surgery.

Before I met with Dr. Smith, I was injected with radioactive dye, a very cool thing to find the lymph nodes. They injected the dye into the tumor area and as it drained from the breast, it stopped in the first lymph node leaving the breast. Then, Dr. Smith used a Geiger counter—sterile, I was assured—to find the radiation-laden lymph node, so they weren't guessing which one was the sentinel node, the one that the breast used for drainage.

The lymph system is very elusive and personal. It seems to be a greatly understudied part of the human anatomy, yet it is crucial for our health and well-being. It is your drainage and filtration system and helps fluids move throughout the body, so they don't get all stuck in one area. With all of the tests that we have today, to the best of my knowledge, there is no scan that will tell what the situation is with your lymph system.

Very shortly after the injection, I was prepping for surgery. They were actually running ahead of schedule. I was a little tearful saying good-bye to my family before surgery. Once again, it was so hard to put my loved ones through this. I saw the care and concern on their faces. They were all so worried; it just ripped out my heart! I had the easy part. I just needed to sleep, and I did it like a champ.

It took a while to emerge from the anesthesia, but once I did, I got to have some Lorna Doones and head home. With some pain meds in hand, my family, my blanket, and I were on our way. There were two incisions, one in the armpit and one on the breast, all covered, with instructions to keep them dry over the next couple of days.

Now guess what—healing and *more waiting*. The next answer we were waiting for was whether the nodes and margins were clean and cancer-free. Not that it really mattered if my nodes were clean. I already knew I was having chemo, so "good news" just meant that it was caught early, for which of course I could thank my husband.

The wait was ridiculous. Surgery was on a Tuesday, and in spite of my calling every other minute, it wasn't until a week and a half later, Sunday morning, December 23, that Dr. Smith called. Yes, Dr. Smith called during her vacation on a Sunday morning. We were impressed.

Pathology was the holdup, and the results were finally reported midday Saturday. Nodes were clean, margins—not so much. Dr. Smith was going to see if radiation would be able to clean up the margins to avoid another surgery, because it was very close to perfect. We got some other information. I zoned out after a minute of technical mumbo jumbo. My husband stayed on task, asking Dr. Smith questions about me, which my head-in-the-sand approach didn't want the answers to.

Two issues I did care about were the lack of range of motion in my arm and the fact that my boob was *enormous*—I am talking double-D big. She said this was normal.

The arm thing is called cording, and I was doing some stretching for it. This is something that is not written about too much, not even on the Internet. The cords were so tight under my arm, I thought I could use them to learn to play the banjo. They ran from the bottom of my armpit straight through so you could actually see them, like clotheslines. Mass General is doing a study on lymphedema and cording, which is more common than one would think. The researcher I spoke with said they saw it in about 60 percent of the cases they were studying, and they were publishing an article on it.

Five minutes after David and I hung up from speaking to Dr. Smith, we decided that I wanted to have another surgery to clean up the margins and not leave it to the radiologist. We'd come this far and waited this long; we might as well do it 100 percent. Every delay pushed chemo closer and closer to my son's May 12 graduation, and I kept refiguring the dates. Once again, I was completely naïve about how long and winding this road would be.

At a lumpectomy follow-up exam, I was referred to a physical therapist to help with my cording and ginormous boob.

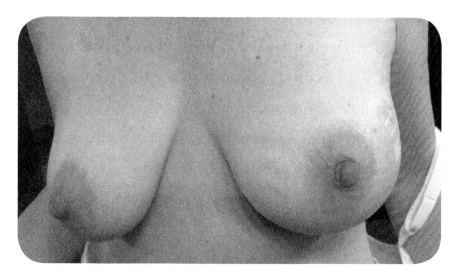

One big scary boob...Post-lumpectomy #1

First the therapist explained how the scar tissue in my armpit and my breast caused kinks in the lymphatic-drainage system. This is actually just a theory because they are unable to really verify the information with any tests. If I *gently* broke up the scar tissue with stretching and massage, it would get better. I figured that if I ignored it, it would get better anyway, but I am a woman of action and wanted it better sooner rather than later.

On the Internet, of the two references that I found for cording, one of them said that the PT that she went to snapped them for instant relief. That's what I expected but was relieved about my course of treatment, because it was far less intense and painful. Then the PT gave me a special large waffle-like cushion to wear in my bra to help with the swollen breast. Although it required some wardrobe adjustments to accommodate this contraption, it worked great. I wore it day and night for about ten days and even though it didn't fix the problem completely, it helped quite a bit.

My family was so supportive of me and helpful in any way they could be. My boys, David Jr. and Doug, decided to get me the ultimate helpful present. For Christmas they gave me a lovely tall glass bong and a plentiful supply of *medical* marijuana. As it turned out, I had never been high. I tried it once in my thirties but saw no results and never bothered to try it again. I never tried it in high school, because my father convinced me that

Christmas 2012 with Doug, me, Anne, Bree, David,
crazy dog Tucker, Justine and David Jr.

getting high killed all of your brain cells, and I did not think that was a good idea.

When I opened the present in the presence of my friend, Anne and her seven-year-old daughter, Brianna, I went into a full dissertation on how it was a beautiful new vase to put flowers in and a year's supply of parsley. When Bree is old enough, I'm sure we will have a very good laugh about that story.

Over the course of the next year, I changed my view on pot. Previously, I had been vehemently opposed to marijuana,

because we were told it was a *gateway drug*, psychologically addictive, and only for druggies. Since Massachusetts has now voted in the use of medical marijuana, and I have seen an enormous surge in research on its effectiveness in pain management and other therapeutic benefits, I now no longer see it as the devil's brew. Don't get me wrong, I still actually have not gotten high, but I no longer judge people who do as I previously had.

Lumpectomy number two was scheduled for January 7. I was by now an old pro and zipped on in for this little cleanup. It was again an afternoon surgery; I think I'd been squeezed in, which was perfect for me. This time surgery was very delayed. I was supposed to have surgery at three and ended up going in about seven thirty. I was a little concerned that this had been a long day for the doctor and staff, but I was assured by a very kind nurse that everyone would be on their game for my procedure. I actually didn't mind surgery being delayed. I didn't think they were just wasting time. I believed that Dr. Smith was giving her previous patient her full attention and all necessary time, and that I would get the same. Luckily, I had left my entourage at home, and my husband was hanging around next door at a bar, having a couple of beers. The longer this cancer thing went on, the more the novelty was wearing off.

Everyone wanted to do something to help. Seeing that only my husband, Justine, and I were at home with crazy schedules, and overall I still felt great, I did not really have any need for numerous cheesy chicken cancer casseroles. A couple friends did bring over dinner on various nights, but the outpouring of support far exceeded the amount of food that the three of us could consume.

That was when it dawned on me that instead of feeding me, we could feed the nurses. After we were informed of my upcoming schedule of thirty chemotherapy treatment days plus thirty radiation days, I was able to make up a sign-up sheet to share via Google docs so that I could bring cookies to the staff who were taking such good care of me.

As the cookie schedule progressed, I found that giving cookies to the receptionist on the oncology infusion desk made quite an impression. After the first couple of times I brought cookies to infusion, I no longer had to show my photo ID, I merely had to pass over a plate of cookies, and they knew just who I was. I don't know for sure but this may even have helped me to secure the private rooms, which were in high demand, and I enjoyed so much.

COOKIES FOR CAREGIVERS

Date of Chemo/Radiation	Cookie Maker!
1/29/2013	Linda…while she still feels like it!
2/12/2013	Michele B
2/26/2013	Maria R (actually Eric)
3/12/2013	Linda B
3/26/2013	Heidi M
4/2/2013	Susan M
4/9/2013	Karyn
4/16/2013	Jennie Lee
4/23/2013	Marilyn
4/30/2013	Michele B
5/7/2013	Heidi W.
5/14/2013	Susan E
5/21/2013	Karyn
5/28/2013	Janice K
6/4/2013	Susan M.
6/11/2013	Meghan
6/18/2013	Me
6/28/13	Sue B
7/9/13	Heidi M
7/23/2013	Marilyn

COOKIES FOR CAREGIVERS

Date of Chemo/Radiation	Cookie Maker!
7/30/2013	Nel
8/6/2013	Linda B
8/13/2013	Linda B
8/20/2013	Justine
8/27/2013	Susan M
9/10/13	Janice K
10/1/13	Michele B, in addition, Mom M made cookies decorated like mice.
10/22/13	Karyn
11/12/13	Jennie Lee
12/3/13	Susan E
12/24/13	Karyn
1/14/13	Heidi M (Just grabbing spots because I'm in baking mode again :-) but I don't mean to hog them all. Feel free to sub your name for mine if you're inclined ;-))
2/4/13	Heidi M (ditto from above)
2/25/13	Heidi M (ditto from above)
3/18/13	Heidi M (ditto from above)

After the first few cookie deliveries, I asked the bakers if they would divide the goodies on two or three plates, so that I could spread the joy throughout my appointments. Dr. Younger, my oncologist, really appreciated the cookies along with Lauren, a wonderful person who was an added benefit I received because of the Pertuzamab (a monoclonal antibody for use in the treatment of HER2+ breast cancer) study. She monitored the testing, scheduling, and side effects of numerous oncology trials. Lauren would visit me regularly during my infusions and was always a ray of sunshine.

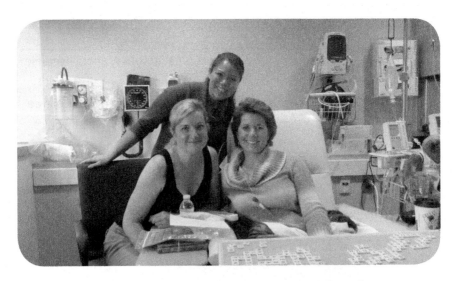

Lauren, Adrianne, and I puzzling away the afternoon!

CHAPTER 4

Starting Chemotherapy!

Someday, in the future, chemotherapy will be looked at the same way we currently look at electric shock therapy. Barbaric! As we progress in understanding cancer and finding treatments, it will eventually be looked back upon as ludicrous that we sat people down weekly and pumped them full of a broad-spectrum poison. *Little soldiers, my ass. It is poison.*

On January 10, I finally saw an oncologist. Over three months post-lump discovery! I was happy in life having a manicurist, hairstylist, massage therapist, but it really stinks to *have* an oncologist. Especially when the oncologist's treatment undoes all of the work of the others.

Good news came out of the exam. Lumpectomy number two yielded clean margins and now I could get on with the fun part: *chemo*. Prior to this meeting, I knew chemo was on the horizon, but frequency and duration haven't been too specifically discussed. The deadline in my mind was still my son's May 12 graduation. The fact that I would probably be wearing a wig to it hadn't really crossed my mind.

I met with Dr. Jerry Younger. He gave me the schedule. AC—Adriamycin (doxorubicin) and Cytoxan (cyclophosphamide)—every other week for four treatments, then Taxol weekly for twelve weeks. And starting the first Taxol week, a special medicine called Herceptin which treated the HER2+ factor. This would be given every three weeks for a year.

I also met Maria, a nurse who would be following my care because of a drug trial I volunteered to take part in. Her role was to monitor me and also to make sure that I fully understood all that was going on. Maria was delightful. She was also due to have a baby any minute. I would miss her for the months that she'd be home with her newborn, but because my regimen was so long I would definitely be seeing her again.

There is a movie called *Living Proof* which really does a great job explaining how Dr. Slamon created his drug that has saved so many lives. Prior to this medication, my prognosis with HER2+ was very (and I mean *very*) grim.

Prior to even starting any infusions, I composed handwritten thank-you cards to both Dr. Slamon and his family, as well as the president and the board of directors of Revlon, Inc. It was important for me to let them know that I appreciated their dedication and financial support that helped get Herceptin to market. To put my money where my mouth is, I purchased some Revlon stock, and I will continue to choose Revlon products over other brands.

During this visit I also learned that I could participate in the study for Pertuzumab, a drug similar to Herceptin from the same company. It was supposed to work also on the HER2+ factor. They needed my permission to send my cancer tumor slides to Germany to verify my HER2+ness to see if I qualified. Honestly, I didn't care what they did with the cancer they cut out of me...

Pertuzumab has helped metastatic patients and is already approved for some uses. Participating in this study was a bonus that I might be getting by choosing to have treatments at Mass General. The reason I only might have been getting this bonus was that it was a double blind study, and I only had a fifty/fifty chance of getting the actual drug and not a placebo. This study was going on all over the world and I felt excited to be part of cancer research. I would not know for three to five years whether I received the drug or the placebo, and then they'd use the information as to whether I'm still here, or perhaps dead, to tell if it worked.

My P? (Pertuzumab or Placebo) drug would be given on the same schedule, every three weeks, as the Herceptin and continue also for a year. The only thing that taking part in the study would cost me was time, and it could increase my chances of survival. I really hoped I'd get the actual drug. I could use all the help I could get.

Being a visual person, I made a poster board chart of all of the treatments that I would be getting. I didn't add any dates, because apparently showing up for a chemo treatment and actually getting one aren't a definite. My daughter decorated it for me with motivational phrases and smiley faces. My first chemo session was scheduled for January 22, 2013. Per the Pertuzumab study, it couldn't start until two weeks after your last surgery. My hopes of treatments being completed prior to my son's graduation were now totally dashed, so it didn't matter when I began. I'd be attending my son's graduation in the midst of chemo treatments wearing a wig. It is as it is. F U, Cancer!

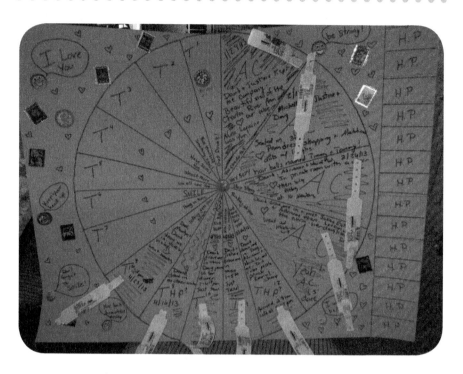

Chemo chart featuring 4 AC treatments,
12 Taxol/Herceptin and P? treatments and 14 more
Herceptin/P? to complete the year.

On January 12, my extended family and lots of long-term friends of my father gathered to celebrate his eightieth birthday. This was something that I would usually orchestrate and speak at—about what an amazing man my father is. On this particular occasion, five days post-surgery and ten days before chemotherapy, I realized that, surrounded by so many loved ones, I was incapable of saying anything without totally breaking down. My love for my father and our very, very close relationship made it impossible for me to speak, because at that point I was not sure I'd outlive him, something that I knew would break his heart. I have always been his quintessential *little girl*.

Seeing that I had a huge chemo regimen in front of me, it was recommended that I have an infusion port installed. On January 15, my husband developed the flu, complete with a 102.5° fever, and couldn't take me to Boston. No worries—my dad was on the job. I was scheduled for a triple header: first, some blood work, then an echocardiogram, and finally the installation of the port. I had my eighty-year-old dad traipsing all over the hospital.

The echocardiogram was required as part of the study, although I would have had it anyway with Herceptin. I'd been told that all of these drugs could really damage the heart. They could kill me while trying to cure me. It was a risk I needed to take. I could live, but live with a damaged heart.

Getting an echocardiogram is pretty cool, aside from the fact that they ask out loud when you check in for your height and weight. I actually asked them for paper and pencil, because this is information I did not want to announce to the entire waiting room. It's bad enough everyone knows how old I am!

The echo is an ultrasound done with the same wand that detected my lump. During the exam I could see my heart pumping, the valves opening and closing, and the blood flowing. Because it was in color, I could see the blood flowing into the heart was a little bluish. Then it would flow out bright red, filled with oxygen. (I think that is what the colors represented, but as I said before, if you actually want true data on this stuff, don't rely on me as a source.)

The thought of the port totally grossed me out. During a chemo class David and I attended with Lorraine, our teacher and subsequent chemo nurse, she explained about the port and the procedure to put it in. The port is installed with two incisions: one just above my right breast and the other on my throat, cutting into my jugular. Apparently they thread a thing into a vein near the jugular so that the medication can flow directly in, just like an IV. The port is like a little dartboard in my chest that protrudes about one-half inch out from my chest wall under the skin. Lorraine said that every chemo nurse on the floor would have one installed if they had to have chemo, because it makes treatments so much easier. If I didn't have the port installed I would need to have an IV put in for every treatment, and the actual nature of the chemo shuts down your veins so it was doubly hard.

The port was installed on my right chest, sort of centered between the top of my shoulder and my breast. The reason that the port is installed on the opposite side from where you have cancer is because when they do radiation, they do not want it to be in the way, especially for those of us who will be having chemotherapy straight through and long after radiation is done.

After the echo, I was summoned to the procedure room for the port installation. A physician's assistant was going to be doing the procedure, observed by a doctor she was going to teach. This seemed backward to me; I would think the doctor would teach the PA.

To top off this backward situation, the PA was the liveliest person I had yet to meet at MGH. She came bouncing in the room full of spunk and energy. She was very thorough and professional, but she was so pretty and cheerful, it was tough to take her seriously. I needed to ask how many of these she had done before she sliced my jugular. At least five hundred was the answer. They do five per day every day of the week. What a sad state of affairs that so many people need these for infusions!

The procedure is done with the patient, a.k.a. me, wide awake. I think I had a little happy juice, but I was definitely awake. I explained to the PA that I was very prone to the low percentage side effects and asked her to please be sure that it was placed securely. As much as I like to keep people entertained, I think that springing a leak from my jugular over dinner would be a little much.

Because of chemo class, we had an insight into a few things that needed to be done prior to my first infusion. One thing was to get my teeth cleaned, because it was dangerous to have them poking around and possibly causing an infection during such a vulnerable time. Something I never thought of was to get a passport picture taken that can be used for passport renewal or license renewal. As it turned out, my passport expired while I was at the peak of baldness and fat as a cow. The last thing I wanted was to look at a picture of myself fat and wigged for the next ten years on my new passport.

I solved the problem by taking an old picture of myself and through a little Photoshop help from my son David turning the background white; it ended up being an acceptable picture. My friend Janice suggested I could always put a horrible picture and then just say I lost it and get a replacement one when I felt better about myself. What a good idea.

So on January 22, my husband, daughter Justine, and I headed into Boston. The whole concept of chemo was very, very scary to me, more because of the unknown than the known. Looking on the bright side of things as always, I hoped to succumb to quite a bit of vomiting and lose the extra ten pounds I'd been struggling with. I always see the glass half full.

I would grow to understand that each chemo routine was the same, no matter which type I was getting. Upon arrival I would head to the eighth floor of the Yawkey building at the Massachusetts General Hospital, which is where the adult infusion unit is. I would check in and take a seat. Most times the wait was not bad, and perhaps only a few times, out of the thirty chemotherapy treatments that I had, did I have to wait a little longer than normal.

A medical assistant came into the waiting room and called me by first name. I then confirmed my date of birth, which apparently is public knowledge, because every place you go, you have to announce it before they'll even take you back. At this point they measured weight, blood pressure, pulse, and oxygen level. I usually went into the treatment area by myself, since the room where they took these measurements was very small, and I worked hard at not letting my husband know my weight.

Shortly after that, when my nurse was available, I returned to the treatment area and my port was accessed. This was done quite quickly, easily, and also pain-free. Lorraine, my nurse, felt my chest to make sure she had the correct location of my port. She then used a bunch of large Q-tips with a special solution to sanitize the area. This is very important, especially if you consider that she was going to be accessing something that goes directly into my bloodstream. She did the procedure wearing special sanitized gloves and a mask to be sure I did not get contaminated. Once the area was sterile, she took a needle that looked like the shape of the number seven and pushed it right into the center of the pincushion. The only pain was a little pinch upon entry through the skin and sometimes a bit of pressure on the chest just from the force of the insertion.

Now that the port was accessed, Lorraine pulled blood out to be sure there was no clot and the flow was good. Then, she took a series of test tubes and filled them for testing, which was done before most treatments.

I was very fortunate that my relationship with Lorraine began before my first day of chemo. Upon entering the treatment ward and seeing each other, we embraced and knew that, although I was there under difficult circumstances, we were going to have a great time!

After the port was accessed, I was instructed to head to the ninth floor of the same building and see Dr. Younger. Dr. Younger evaluated the blood tests and made sure I was ready to roll. As expected, because prior to this I was healthy as a horse except for a little cancer, all of my numbers were good. Of course, I was already a little disappointed that my weight was so high, thanks to that stupid pill, but some things can't be helped. My weight was used to determine the chemotherapy formula, which was adjusted, if needed, before every infusion.

After I got the green light to go ahead with my first treatment, we headed back down to the eighth floor and checked in again. I gave Lorraine the cookies I baked for the chemo nurses and got seated in what I affectionately referred to as the penthouse suite. This is an area with two treatment chairs and the most amazing view of the city of Boston overlooking the Charles River. It was bright and sunny but also freezing cold. For some reason they can't get the heat to work well in this area, perhaps because of all the glass.

As my treatments went on, time after time, I developed more and more knowledge of how the system worked. I learned that at check-in, I could request a private room. These rooms did not have the spectacular vista that the penthouse did, but they were better for me, as I preferred privacy. I am a very, very loud person, and I usually had a lot of company. Although I liked to party through each chemo treatment, there were those who preferred the quieter approach to treatment, and I did not want to disturb them.

So, I finished my first chemo treatment and stayed in Boston for a nice dinner. Now the scarier part: what to expect when we got home?

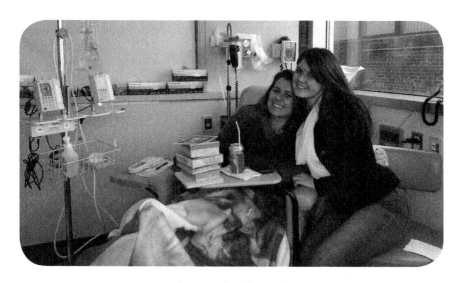

Justine and I on the first day of chemo

Prior to leaving my first treatment, Lorraine wrote out a very detailed list of medications that I was going to be taking at a certain time. Because of another miracle drug, Emend, an anti-nausea drug that is given through IV prior to starting the AC treatment, it appeared that I would not be spending the majority of my time vomiting. On my list of at-home medications were Zofran, as needed for vomiting; Decadron, a steroid to help my body protect itself; Compazine, another medication to prevent vomiting; and Ativan every four to six hours to help me relax and sleep while all of these medications and the chemo wreaked havoc on my body.

In addition to this, I was given an extremely expensive injection of a med called Neulasta about twenty-four hours after treatment. The cost of this is $4,000 per shot. Thank God I did not change to the cheaper insurance when I was thinking about it last year. They were delivered to me on ice a few days before my first treatment and needed to be stored in the refrigerator.

As all of this cancer stuff was starting and progressing, my daughter was in her senior year of high school in Worcester, and at some point the thought of her going to college for nursing entered the picture. By the time I had my first treatment, she found out she was admitted to Regis College in Weston for nursing and was very excited about her new career.

All right, I had the shots in the refrigerator but no clue how those were actually going to get into my body, as I am not the kind of person who likes anything to do with the medical profession. Prior to my current position in real estate management, I was a nursing home administrator out of college, but that was a paper-pushing position, not a needle-pushing position. I called my friend Janice, a nurse, and asked her if she would come up and give me the injection and teach Justine how to do it. She was more than happy to accommodate and quite frankly Justine was a little bit too excited about torturing her mother in this way. It looked like she picked the right profession.

With all of the drugs in my system, I slept for a solid three days. We termed this the "chemo coma." This is much better than the old days of throwing up for days on end. Scientists are so amazing that they continually come up with more and more ways to treat medical problems. You never really can appreciate this, until they've created something that will either save your life or make your quality of life better.

The highlight after I emerged from my three days of sleep was seeing my friend Michelle's smiling face. She was holding a bag of my favorite food, crab rangoon. She always knows how to make me feel better.

CHAPTER 5

Naming My Hairballs

It is my opinion that a bald woman is not beautiful. She is sick. She has cancer. If your goal is for everyone at the grocery store and CVS to know you have cancer, a bald head or a scarf will do the trick. Sometimes I do think that it would be nice for a total stranger to look at me with those sympathetic eyes or give me the better parking space because I have a scarf on my head, but that just isn't me. My friend Nancy suggested that there might be days I just didn't feel well enough to wear a wig.

My thought was that if I didn't feel well enough to slap a wig on my head, I truly didn't feel well enough to go out.

At this point, only my husband had seen my pathetic, scraggly head. It has been four weeks since my first chemo treatment. Between treatments two and three of AC, we went to Florida and were houseguests at my sister-in-law's and then my father's. During that time, I wore a wig anytime I was out of my bedroom. It wasn't for me but for them. This whole thing makes people sad. To see me with 95 percent of my hair missing would make this thing that I had only talked about very real. People who love me were already sad enough about my health situation. If I could go through this whole thing and spare my husband the pain of seeing me look like a *cancer patient*, I would, but unfortunately I couldn't shower or sleep in my wigs. Wearing a wig all the time protected the people I love from the truth of my situation.

On Monday, two weeks after my first treatment of AC, more hair than usual was falling out. On Tuesday, Timmy and Tommy, two rodent hair balls, were at the shower drain. On Wednesday, I started texting pictures of hair balls to my friends. One friend said it was no longer a rodent, more like a small pony.

The names that came back were Rooter, because that is who would need to retrieve it from down the drain, Cheech and Chong (Are we dating ourselves?), and Tom and Jerry.

Yes, it is disgusting. Cancer isn't pretty.

Because of my preemptive nature, I was wig ready from the get-go. My health insurance reimbursed for one wig "prosthetic" per calendar year, and knowing what I was facing, I opted to use my 2012 five hundred dollar allowance in December for my tramp wig. This would be my blonde bombshell wig for the days I just wanted to be someone else.

I made an appointment, assembled a selection of wine, cheese, crackers, and Christmas cookies and eight friends, and we all converged on a wig center in Worcester. Unfortunately, the proprietor wasn't comfortable with my turning this medically necessitated appointment into a fiesta, so the wine had to be left chilling in the frosty New England car for now. I tried on about fifteen wigs, attempting to find ones that were as different from me as possible. My group of friends kept circling back to what wigs looked nice and somewhat normal on me, but my girlfriend's daughter, Hilary, did the best to keep us on track until we found the perfect wig. It was long and blonde—a look I'd never had.

Shortly after the New Year, another smaller wig contingent was formed, and we went to the Salon at 10 Newbury Street in Boston for a wig consultation. I heard about this salon from a friend of mine who got a hair piece from them after she lost a lot of her hair due to toxic shock syndrome.

My "tramp" wig, Miranda, named after my favorite childhood book <u>*Miranda's Beautiful Dream.*</u>

The Salon at 10 Newbury was where I was going to get the *real* Linda wig. Real hair that I could don and look exactly like me. A look that wouldn't leave questions on the mouths of people I knew who didn't know. This place was very nice, and we ordered a wig to be picked up in a couple of days. At the initial meeting, it was fun to pick the color, but returning by myself a couple of days later lost its joy...I clearly needed my support staff to keep me laughing through these more dramatic phases.

When I was shopping for the Linda hair with my wonderful friends, I was able to focus more on the fun and less on the actual situation. As wonderful as they were at 10 Newbury, being there by myself on a Saturday morning made me very sad. I don't usually consider myself to be a needy person, but clearly certain situations having special people as distractions really do help you get through.

The people at 10 Newbury are extremely professional. You can tell they deal with this type of situation all of the time.

The owner, Patricia, is a wonderful person and has formed http://www. wigsforwellbeing.org/ a nonprofit organization that helps people with hair loss obtain wigs. It is nice to

The Linda wig from 10 Newbury Salon in Boston

know that there is a way for everyone in need of a wig to get one.

So, with two wigs in hand, I thought I was all set until another friend dropped off her redheaded wig for me to use since she was through with her battle with ovarian cancer. Now I had, in the words of our friend John, a full Napoleon ice cream of wigs—chocolate, strawberry, and vanilla!

So, how traumatic is it to lose your hair? Not as bad as I thought it would be. From the first day I had less hair than I wanted, I flipped on the Miranda wig and my sunglasses and went about my day. This was the day I saw my son in Richmond and my in-laws in North Carolina and my sister-in-law in Florida, and nobody missed a beat. I think it all came from my attitude. I truly wasn't bothered by the hair loss and the wig. It was just a necessary accessory to get me to become healthy and whole again. I was told that my hair would probably grow in gray, and curly but that will need to be a chapter all by itself.

CHAPTER 6

I'm on the Wagon

If I recall correctly, the last time I was on the wagon was when I had buns in the oven. Here again, something was growing inside me, and now I needed a drink more than ever, and I was going cold turkey. This was by choice. The advice from the chemo class was not to drink forty-eight hours before or forty-eight hours after an infusion to help your liver do its job. I figure if less alcohol would help, none would be even better for me.

Beginning Sunday night, January 27, before my first Tuesday chemo, I enjoyed copious amounts of white zinfandel as my last hurrah! I felt bad for Beringer and Sutter Home—their stocks might take a hit over the next few months without me partaking of their goodness in my three- to four-night-a-week indulgence.

The real problem without drinking isn't giving it up as much as what to drink instead. Part of my weight loss management system is not to drink any calories unless they are cream in my coffee, or they contain alcohol. This would be fine, because I could proceed on to Diet Coke, but that would have me gazing at the ceiling with insomnia at three in the morning because of the caffeine. And for some reason I can never understand, aside from an occasional diet root beer, which I really don't care for, there is no diet caffeine-free soda served at restaurants—like it violates an unwritten rule. Would I be asking too much for a Diet Sprite, caffeine-free Diet Coke or a diet ginger ale? I remember the same problem when I was nursing babies and couldn't find a calorie-free drink to enjoy.

So ice water with lemon became my go-to beverage, until our friend John forbade me to have bar fruit, a haven of bacteria after being left open on the bar all day, after being manhandled when it is cut up, and repeatedly picked through for each beverage. Yuck! Now I would never have bar fruit again, even after

I was better. And to think I was the kind who always ate it and considered it part of my daily allowance of fruits and vegetables. Luckily Nancy saved the day by suggesting carrying Crystal Light or another of those water flavorings, and it did the trick. I was being good—my liver only had to decontaminate the drugs from Mass General, and I was feeling great, so I would probably stay on the wagon, at least until the Taxol cleared my system.

CHAPTER 7

Sex and Chemo— a Toxic Combination?

If you can sense a red glow over Massachusetts, it is my husband's face glowing red at the mere thought that someone is reading this chapter. Prior to my friend Nancy's harebrained idea for me to write this book, my husband preferred to keep a low profile and lead a nonpublic life. I have always been the one to let it all hang out and tell it like it is. (Let's face it, the first picture in this book is of my boobs!) It is really embarrassing how many stories and opinions I like to share. Hopefully my friends know it is always good spirited.

So anyway, about sex. It was different. The first hiccup in our regular routine was that upon learning I had a positive hormone receptive cancer, I had to discontinue the use of Seasonique, an awesome pill that gave me just four periods a year. I loved it. As I was also getting closer to menopause, I was thinking I could just sail right through with this pill and wake up one day period-free without a hot flash in sight! In addition, I heard that the birth control pill actually helps prevents ovarian cancer. Oops, wrong cancer. Did this pill cause my cancer? The thought had crossed my mind, but my feeling was no. I put a hundred chemicals on and in my body every day, whether it is my shampoo, cream rinse, or coffee. I think it would be impossible to point a finger at just one thing that caused this f**king cancer.

Just as a side note: Dr. Dunn explained to me when I went on the pill that because the pill prevents ovulation, it actually is helpful in preventing ovarian cancer. This is because every time you ovulate, the surface of your ovary has a cyst rupture to release the egg. If you are on the pill, then you do not have this rupture and egg release. Cancer is a mutated cell that happens during the work repairing the cyst area; therefore, every ovulation and subsequent repair of the ovarian surface is a potential problem or area of concern. Once again, my disclaimer—if you actually want the facts of what I am talking about, you should research it yourself. I cannot be held responsible for the multitude of misinformation I am providing.

So now I had periods, and I had lost my backup birth control method. The trial I was in for Pertuzamab required that a barrier method needed to be used during sexual intercourse. I thought this was probably overkill, since my husband (who you can probably feel blushing) had a vasectomy after our daughter was born. That, however, was almost eighteen years ago, and now I was freaked out. I had no idea if "Fred" was still shooting blanks and needed to find out right away. After a few phone calls, I found out I needed a urologist to run the sample for us. Quite frankly, as I went through all of this, I was thinking, "I can handle cancer, but I could not handle having to have an abortion because I got pregnant during chemo." I can handle a lot, but that is one thing that would have killed me on the inside for the rest of my life.

We learned more about the fun we would have with sex from our chemo class teacher and nurse, Lorraine. She and I hit it off right away. She went over the dos and don'ts and some things we will cover later, but the sex portion caught both my husband's and my attention. The barrier method was not just to prevent pregnancy, but also to prevent the chemicals that were making my hair fall out and killing every fast-growing cell in my body from causing Mr. Winky to fall off. Now this was serious! So an immediate question popped into our minds...Oral? Lorraine, quick on her feet said, "Saran wrap." It might be worth a try.

Proactively, as I had been with every step of this journey, I swung through CVS like a horny teenager and bought a variety pack of condoms, since I had no clue what I was doing. I wasn't sure I'd ever had the job to buy the condoms, and if I did, it was over twenty-five years ago. I was surprised how many choices there are and also how expensive. But as I have told my own kids, it's cheaper than the alternative!

My husband was willing to let me extract a seminal sample—really, what man says no to a blow job? But his cooperation stopped there because he refused to come to the appointment at the urologists. I felt like an idiot showing up with his sample in a reusable Glad container in a little bag. The receptionist had set up an appointment for the doctor to see the source whence the sample came, but I explained it was all I could do to get him to cooperate and give the sample. He refused to come to the appointment.

I could talk in a deep voice and answer the questions if it would help the situation. After much ado, they took the sample and said to call in twenty-four hours. I'm sure the fact that I used the "I have cancer card" and really can't get pregnant, helped.

My husband got the results the next day. There were no fishies swimming in the sea. What a relief! Almost forty-eight years old, nearly empty nesting, and sick with cancer, a baby would not be the best blessing right now.

Changes abound! First off, titties were fun. Clearly from the beginning of this book they got regular attention and were a part of our repertoire. Now the left one was cut up from two lumpectomies and the right one had a port just above it that connected to my jugular (every mention of that curdles my stomach). So those areas went from high-priority fun centers to almost nil. My dear husband did try to work around those issues, so I didn't feel bad about myself. I knew that the port would be out in a year, and shaking up a routine can be okay once in a while.

Something we didn't expect was that all my fluids were all toxic smelling and harsh. Really quite disgusting. There was syrupy fluid leaking from the corner of my eyes, so you can just imagine what it was coming from other places. Even saran wrap couldn't help this situation.

I won't get into any other details, or my husband would put the kibosh on this whole chapter. This was just one of the many bumps that this lump threw our way. My advice (which I have tons of) is still to have lots of sex, even if you need to work hard to get in the mood. There are many lotions and potions and toys to help you along. My friend Nancy works for one of these companies, and discreetly sold me some items to enhance the situation since the saran wrap was better in theory than in practice.

CHAPTER 8

My Husband

Who knew in May 1984, when I locked eyes with this man in our late teens, that all the love and power of love at first sight (on my part, at least) would come to fruition. I grabbed him young, but it took a lot of work to get him properly trained (although he informs me I was no picnic at the beginning myself).

We were the yin and yang of all marriages; he was always full of dreams and adventure and looking forward to the next step, and I was securely the ball and chain of reality. No, we shouldn't move to Montana just because the air is cleaner, we would miss our families...etc. We have had highs and lows like all marriages. Raising our children, we agree, is the ultimate high, and the best thing that our marriage has given the world.

When I got the diagnosis, I had my doubts about how David was going to rise to this occasion. During my labor with our third child, he read a book and ate a cheeseburger instead of rubbing my back and giving me ice chips. He informed me that he had already been through this two times and saw it was pretty easy for me. My routine medical complications of life were not David's best moments, but he jumped right on board the cancer train and became the engineer. He read and researched and consumed everything he could to fully understand what *we* were facing. Having him take the lead made going on this unexpected trip an easier ordeal.

After I recovered from my third bout of A/C chemo, David went up for a couple of nights of skiing with his brothers. Here is what I found on my phone at my two a.m. potty run.

E-mail received March 2:

> *It's 1:00 a.m., and I am just lying down to sleep. I am reflecting about our life. Mostly good times come to mind... very few bad. I can't even remember the manush we may have spat over...*

All I know is that after twenty-seven-plus years, I still love you.

I feel confident that you are going to be a survivor in this fight. But please know...if the worst was to happen, I will be with you always...propping you up to see every last sunset from your bedroom window, white zin in one hand and my hand in the other.

I love you bud...

I am not that prone to crying, but this type of compassion and love really hit home. I really hoped it didn't get to this point, but it was nice to know that he would be here for me, serving me wine in bed.

From the time that my diagnosis was confirmed until my last treatment, David regularly informed our friends and family via e-mail updates about my condition. He mentioned upcoming treatments, as well as circulating the chemo cookie chart, so that people could sign up.

Here are three examples of the numerous e-mails that David sent over the year and a half.

From: David Murphy
Sent: Tuesday December 11, 2013 10:50 P.M.
Subject: Linda Update 12/11/12

Hi All,

Well, here is the report from surgery today. She came through her lobotomy, I mean lumpectomy, just fine... albeit a little sleepy. Her dad, our wonderful dear friend Marilyn, Justine, and I kept the waiting room filled with great banter and wonderful levity which passed the time effortlessly for all of us. Three generations of support.

She is up in bed now, tucked in tight in an OxyContin-aided slumber as I type.

Step one of the journey has now passed!

We will now wait until the pathology report comes back to see if she has clean margins, i.e., the surgeon got all the tumor. We should know the results within ten days. Oh, great, more waiting. If her margins are clean (75 percent chance) then on to the next step, if not then she will go back for another surgery.

Now we wait four to eight weeks until she starts her chemotherapy and Herceptin to try to kill, or at least stop the further growth of, any of the cancer cells that may have scooted away to another part of Linda's body. Her oncology team will come up with a cocktail of chemo just right for her, as there are different concoctions that go with the Herceptin. She is hoping they opt for a Stoli cosmo IV, but that might not be the drug of choice here.

She is upbeat and has even been eyeing a couple of snazzy wigs so she can keep up her party-girl lifestyle! Personally, I am torn between the blonde and the redhead.

As previously stated in past e-mails, Linda is SO VERY BLESSED to have so many wonderful people in her life who care about her. The many, many acts of kindness, be it a simple text of love, the random e-mail of support, so many beautiful cards of well wishes, to those overwhelmingly thoughtful personalized expressions of comfort that are so very touching to her. I know all this outpouring has truly enabled Linda to face this challenge with such optimism so as to overcome this hurdle. Thank you all very much.

Just to illustrate the type of person Linda is. She went out yesterday, unbeknownst to us, and shopped for snacks, drinks, and magazines and made a waiting room goodie bag with something special for each member of her entourage sitting in the waiting room...she has cancer and is going into surgery and all she thinks of is others... That IS Linda.

I will update you all when we have pertinent news to share.

Please feel free to e-mail any questions you may have

and you may share this e-mail with anyone who you think
may have an interest.

My very best to you all and THANK YOU!!
David Murphy

From: David Murphy
Sent: Thursday, January 10, 2013 8:27 P.M.
Subject: Linda Update 1/10/13

Hi All,

Well, we spent the afternoon at Mass General today,
Thursday, meeting with a slew of doctors and other health-
care providers. Linda got the news that her second surgery
was a success, as the sample came back with clean margins.
Now she can proceed with her treatments. The following
course of action was mapped out.

Next week, routine prechemo testing...bone scan, echo-
cardiogram, installing her chemo port...blah blah blah...

In about two weeks she starts her five months of chemo-
therapy, made up of two months of Adriamycin & Cytoxan
given every two weeks followed by three months of Taxol
and Herceptin given every two weeks.

She will be getting Herceptin every three weeks for the
remainder of the year.

Four to six weeks after she is done with the chemo, she

will do the six weeks of daily radiation. She will also take Tamoxifen for five to ten years.

An overwhelming day it was, to say the least.

Linda also decided to take part in a drug trial for a chemo drug given every three weeks for a year along with the Herceptin. This drug is called Pertuzumab. There are 3800 woman around the world in the trial. Half will get the drug and half will get a placebo. We won't know which group she was in until three to five years from now.

Again, I thank each and every one of you for being so kind and concerned about Linda.

I have shared all the nice e-mails I receive back from you all with Linda, and it warms her heart.

She is a very special and positive woman who will conquer this battle.

My Best,

David Murphy

From: David Murphy
Sent: Jun 12, 2013, at 6:02 P.M.
Subject: Linda Update 6/12/13

Hello Gang,

I hope this update note finds you all happy and healthy.

Linda passed another hurdle yesterday. She has had

ten of twelve weekly Taxol chemotherapy treatments, and yesterday was to be the eleventh. It was canceled by the oncologists at MGH due to the fact that Linda has been experiencing too much pain from the nerve damage from the Taxol resulting in neuropathy in her hands and feet as well and toenail loss. It was decided that the risk/reward was too great to continue with any more Taxol, so that portion of her treatment is now over. This is very good news, as this batch of chemo has really accumulated some uncomfortable side effects for her. As she has said, "This is getting very old."

Now she settles into her Herceptin, coupled with the trial drug (or placebo) chemotherapy every third Tuesday until next March/April 2014. This type of chemo is called a monoclonal antibody-targeted therapy and has very little side effects. After Herceptin will come ten years of Tamoxifen.

The radiologist recommends that Linda's body have ample time to recuperate and get stronger before her radiation phase of treatment. Therefore, her start date for radiation is July 22nd. Which of course messed up the cookie schedule which can be adjusted below. She will get a twenty-second zap each weekday for six weeks. It has been told to her that after the long dose of various chemo that she has already had radiation will be a cake walk. We hope to make the best of it and spend some time exploring Boston during this treatment.

A special thank you to the cookie brigade. The staff are all so grateful. The response each week is so positive and spreads joy both to the staff and Linda to be able to make them happy!

Last night she jumped off the wagon and whooped it up with some good friends at Funky Murphy's and cut loose. I was on edge with caution and concern, as I was not sure how the copious glasses of wine were going to affect her after all the crap that has flowed through her body for the last five months...but all was well. What a trooper!! She even got up at 7 A.M. and went to meet some workmen at the property she manages.

So, at this juncture we continue on this ride, and although we wish this was not happening to her, we are blessed to have so very many wonderful, supportive, caring, and giving friends and family. The outpouring of acts of love by so many of you has been nothing short of overwhelming. We want to thank each of you, and you know who you are, for all you have done.

Linda's hair and nails should be slowly returning to normal over the next year to year and a half, but I will be still looking forward to the occasional night with Miranda or Ginger when Linda is not around. We are hoping that the neuropathy will subside over this time as well, as it is such a nuisance to the "energizer bunny."

So, to wrap this up, let us hope that all the little critters who may have left the barn are dead, and if not, the last few will meet their demise over the balance of Linda's treatments and she will go on to live a full life with no reoccurrence.

Feel free to pass this on to whoever you feel may have any interest.

Until next time.....Be well, our friends!

My Best,

David Murphy

These updates were so helpful in alleviating the need to continually repeat the same information over and over again. It was difficult enough to be "living" the situation, and it was helpful not to have to continue to "relive" it. Due to my "the cup is always half-full" philosophy and optimistic personality, I tended to only share a rose-colored story anyway. It was only a select few who were privy to the true trials and tribulations I was experiencing.

CHAPTER 9

. . . .

Wahhh, Wahhh, Wahhh

Yeah! My last AC treatment was Tuesday, March 19.
I was so glad I got that done and now could move
on. On my usual schedule, I got blood drawn from
my port by Lorraine; then got the thumbs up from
oncology that my levels were all on track and to cook
up my chemo. With cookies in hand, thanks to my
dear friends—one of whom, Linda B, actually wrote
a letter to the nurses thanking them for taking such
great care of me (it was a real tearjerker). We started
my final one of the tough

treatments. My rock, David, brought me in, and my friends Susan E and Adrianne joined the party. We got a private room, and the day went quickly. The private room allowed me to Skype with my mother-in-law during treatment. During each of these chemo sessions one thing remained unchanged. The more the merrier, and being surrounded by wonderful friends and family really made things go quickly and more bearable!

We got out and home before rush hour, which was a treat for this treatment. Starting Wednesday morning, I slipped into my chemo coma, a blessing, if the alternative was being nauseated. The main problem with the chemo coma was my brain was so fuzzy. When your brain turns to mush, it can be quite frustrating. In addition to mashed-potato brain, this round of chemicals resulted in my becoming a puddle of tears for two days. Sad? No, I wasn't sad; I just cried and cried and cried. I pretty much cried all day Friday and all day Saturday. Deciding what to eat for lunch resulted in sobs, and discussing what the menu should be for the family Easter dinner got me crying hysterically (funny how it appears that all I thought about was food). Because previously, I was out of my coma by Friday afternoon, well-wishers called, and stupidly I would answer the phone and sob to anyone who was checking on my status—clearly my status wasn't very good.

Luckily, I woke up Sunday morning back to 95 percent of my old self. One of the problems with this was that all the calls that I took and e-mails that I sent and replied to should have been substantially edited. I now realize that someone should have removed all of my technology until I had totally resurfaced. Never mind how badly I did taking my turn with Words with Friends. True friends wouldn't let me play with chemo brain.

On Sunday we decided to have a little getaway and visit David's sister, Dianne. Turned out that during our stay, I got a bug, and with the lower immune system it got the best of me. I had a fever and after hours of my stomach hurting and gurgling, I vaulted for the toilet. I sort of made it but not before throwing up all over my sister-in-law's dry-clean-only linen shower curtain. Figured I would be in one of the only bathrooms in the United States with a decorative shower curtain that needed to be dry cleaned. Dianne's house is so well decorated, and she is such an amazing hostess, that I think Martha Stewart calls her for decorating and entertaining tips.

Sheepishly, my husband balled up the shower curtain and left it with a note and fifty dollars for the dry-cleaning bill. Needless to say, I was probably the worst houseguest she ever had. Once again, the worst part of having cancer is making people sad. My being sick with a fever and vomiting did just that to my husband and daughter, and all of the in-laws who were also visiting.

Prior to my mishap in the bathroom, the fever prompted a call to Dr. Jerry Younger, because we had been instructed to call if I had a fever over 100.5°. The weakened immune system can require a trip to the hospital to get additional medications to fight a virus that most people can handle without a problem. My husband, whom Dr. Younger remembered better than me because he asked all the questions and knew what was going on, was instructed to give me some Tylenol, and if my fever didn't go down to head to the emergency room. Luckily, the fever went down a bit and stayed there with regular medicine, and I dodged a trip to the ER. A small victory!

AC really bites. It kicked my butt in many ways over two months. I was fortunate to feel pretty good in between chemo comas, but I was glad that it was over. Now on to the next round of chemos.

CHAPTER 10

Using the Cancer Card

From the first day that I found out I had cancer and told the kids, I explained to them they have a new "buy" to get out of sticky situations: the cancer card. It was a way to be able to retake a test, miss a class, or get out of any other situation that stopped all arguments in their tracks.

My son, David, was trying to get home on Thursday night for March vacation, and they slipped a midterm into a slot that interfered with his flight home. It was my forty-eighth birthday as well. The e-mail to the professor about how important it was to get home for his mom's birthday, especially because she was in the middle of chemotherapy did the trick. He was able to take the exam a couple of hours earlier and made his flight.

I have used the cancer card myself to tame my difficult tenants. I have a tenant in an office building I manage who fabricates problems for attention. His favorite area of harassment over the winter is snow removal. Until this point, I had not told any of my tenants about my situation. I still had my hair, and my work hours were variable, so as long as I did my job no one was the wiser.

This particular tenant is unreasonable. We live in New England—It snows. If it is snowing, there will be some on the parking lot and sidewalks at any given time. Snowplows remove the snow after a period of time and an amount has accumulated. It is not called snow catching, where you prevent the snow from touching the ground. If you choose to head out, and it's snowing, wear your boots and be careful.

Anyway, this tenant e-mailed me that an employee slipped, fell, and was injured in the parking lot because of the snow. I promptly replied with concern and multiple questions to get the details, including whether or not the person was taken to the hospital via ambulance or car and their contact information. The tenant told me they weren't going to pursue the issue at this time, and wouldn't tell me who the person was.

Knowing this tenant, I realized that it was merely a fictitious story to keep me on my toes. I visited him that afternoon and closed the office door. I told him I had a very aggressive cancer and was doing the best I could. I hired a snow removal company, and they were doing a good job, but because of having cancer treatments, I wasn't able to be here to catch each snowflake as it fell. Oddly, I welled up as I told my story, and he did too...I guess he does have a heart. Since I told him I have cancer, he has been behaving.

Another tenant was also a complainer, and I used my diagnosis to quash her rants about her own problems. She actually changed gears right away and sent me a card out of concern.

My husband has also used the cancer card to control the unruly tenant. One of his tenants kept complaining about his neighbor walking with a heavy step. He dropped the "we all have to deal with something—my wife has cancer," and that put things in perspective for them.

I was waiting for the moment when I needed to cut a line or get out of a sticky situation and pop off my wig to show my nearly (I had about a hundred hairs left on my head as of mid-April) bald head to prove that I had cancer and needed a special favor. I was not sure I would ever actually have the guts to do this, but I was ready if the situation arose.

CHAPTER 11

Fun with Hair

Thousands and thousands of dollars... that is what
I have spent over the years to get hair taken off my
body. I have been shaved, waxed, electrolysized,
plucked, and lasered. When I was younger I suffered
the effects of polycystic ovarian disease and had
a full beard and mustache. It was so pronounced
that the very sweet gentlemen in my middle school
nicknamed me "Linda with the 'Stache." They even
addressed me like that in my eighth-grade yearbook.
Now I was bald like a plucked chicken.

After four AC treatments and after my sixth round of Taxol, I was 99.5 percent bald, eyelashless, eyebrowless, and was even treated to a free Brazilian! This would be great news for my legs and armpits if I hadn't already had all of that hair lasered off. I had gotten rid of all the hair that I didn't want already, and now I was losing the stuff that I wanted to keep. The only area of me that was hairless that I enjoyed was my face. I had a lot of peach fuzz on my face, and the smoother hairless face looked younger. I could enjoy that while it lasted.

I used to be an Italian gorilla. If my life chose a different path I would have had a job with the carnival as the hairiest woman alive. Now I longed for this hair. The only things I did bald were sleep, shower, and exercise.

Before leaving my bedroom each morning, I plopped a wig on my bald crown to head down and make my green tea, which by the way, my own study proves does not prevent cancer. When I finish the BJ's-size box I bought before this all started, I am never drinking it again. I wore a wig so my family could forget that I had cancer, and it wasn't screaming in their face.

Before I left the house, I fully dressed and "haired" myself. This got to be a lot of work. The wig was the easy part. I filled in my eyebrows with a stencil pattern and a special brush and Revlon eyebrow powder. These came out pretty good. To be honest I was touching up my eyebrows before this all began, because they were turning gray. Now they were gone, so the need was more urgent.

The eyelashes were the big challenge. They were a real pain. You could stick them on or glue them. The first time I used the glue, I had visions of myself calling 911 with my eyelids glued shut, explaining that they had to take me to the hospital because I couldn't drive because I couldn't see. In spite of this vision, I did try the glue. Yuck! It had a chemical smell, ruined the eyelash set, and when it dried it had a sharp edge that annoyed me all day.

The pair of Revlon eyelashes (from the company whose donation to Dr. Slamon probably saved my life, I hope) were easy to use. I just peeled them off the plastic and stuck them on. You also got an extra strip to use them again. Because of the regular usage I actually found replacement strips, so I could keep using the same pair of eyelashes. I found them on the Internet. These Fabulash strips were a little bit labor intensive but more economical and worked out pretty well. I bought a sixty-day supply, so I was set for a while. If I traveled at all, I bought more Revlon lashes, so I didn't need to spend all morning in the bathroom fighting with the strips.

If I was in the mood to get a little recognition and sympathy,

I switched my wigs up often, and when someone noticed my frequent change in hairstyle, I'd tell them it was a wig. Everyone knew why a forty-something-year-old was wearing a wig. Some people would say, "May I ask why?" and some people just said, "Oh, I had no idea. I am so sorry." Occasionally, people just guessed the type, "Breast?" Of course this circled right back to the stories. As soon as I shared what I was going through—and it did feel good to get it off my chest once in a while for a little "there, there" from people I knew, the stories began.

The good news about this is that I was not alone. The bad news is that everyone's life is touched by cancer.

One day my daughter and husband wanted to go parasailing. An activity I love, but knew I couldn't do in my wigged state. Nevertheless, I decided to join them for the boat ride. The joke was on me, as the captain floored the boat, and my wig began to lift. I quickly resecured it, tethered the longer strands of my Miranda wig under my chin, and held my wig in place like a bonnet. I needed a scarf like one would wear in a fifties movie to keep my hair in place. When I was trying to take pictures of the event, I had the person I was with place her hand on my head, so I could snap a few photos without feeding the fish a synthetic meal.

Because I never had a wig before, the care of it was a little

confusing. The wigs did not need to be washed except after every ten to fourteen wearings. This seemed like a long time to me, but there really was not any reason to do it earlier if the wig still looked good. The real-hair wig, after it is washed, needed to be treated with styling product, blown dry, and styled. This was easier said than done, because it was hard to do it on your head, but even harder to do it on a Styrofoam head. Somehow I muddled through, and most of the time it looked pretty good.

The synthetic wig was actually a little bit more difficult because it got easily matted and snarled. Someone told me to use laundry fabric softener on it after I washed it, and that trick helped a lot. The benefit of the synthetic wig was that it was much less expensive, and I did not need to style it but merely let it hang to dry. I usually combed it through with the fabric softener on it before rinsing it and leaving it to dry.

Two things that made a big difference in the comfort of the wigs were clips and getting it properly sized. Both of my wigs were purchased while I still had a full head of hair. You might think that that would not throw off the size of the wig, but it does. I still had about half of my hair when I started to wear wigs, and there were neat little clips sewn into the wig to secure it on to my thinning hair. This was just enough so that it did not slide off, and it was quite secure. When I was almost completely bald, I snipped out the clips because they were very scratchy on my head.

I returned to both of the places where I bought the wigs and they were kind enough to resize them for me since I needed them much smaller for comfort and security.

A couple of months after my last Taxol treatment, I returned to 10 Newbury Street, and Pat sewed clips back into my wings so they could grip my half inch of gray frizzy chemo-curl Afro.

CHAPTER 12

Everyone Has a Story!

Just like pregnancy, if you have cancer, everyone is very excited to share their personal experience.

"I am being treated for cancer." This was the wording I used, because I did not feel like I had cancer. I had a little bit of cancer in my boob, and Dr. Smith cut it out. Because of the HER2+ I was having chemo because even though the lymph nodes were clean, a crazy over-producing HER2+ cell might have escaped, and the chemo was my life insurance policy.

The response was almost always the same—my friend, my sister, my mother, or I—had cancer. It was always in the past tense, and apparently I looked like I cared and wanted to hear the story.

One of the key elements of all breast cancer stories is that the person that they know is fine, and I will be too. This was one of the reasons that people are sure I will be fine. They know someone who also had breast cancer and is fine. I am also assured that being a strong person and having a positive attitude cures cancer. This is very good news for me. I am both.

Well, I'd "had cancer" officially since November and was growing annoyed by the cancer stories. Mainly the breast cancer stories. I felt like anyone who had any cancer and had surgery alone or surgery with radiation had "cancer lite." For these people, the whole ordeal was usually wrapped up in three or four months and they could get on with life.

I am sorry to downplay anyone who has had cancer, but there are definitely different degrees of cancer. I feel like mine is in the middle of "cancer lite," and what I was going through couldn't even compare to serious, metastasized cancer.

The way it works for the general public is that a cancer survivor is a cancer survivor, but I really have to disagree. If you have sat in the infusion unit week after week and month after month, hearing and seeing the other patients struggle with frequent infusions, wigs, bald heads, helmets, in wheelchairs, on oxygen, a child in a wagon, and an IV bag hanging, you would know that all cancer isn't created equal.

Being diagnosed with cancer is scary! I feel sure that each and every diagnosed person knows that having cancer can be a death sentence, and at the beginning of every journey through cancer a person is fearful of the process and the outcome. That being said, if the journey from diagnosis to *cure* is only a couple of months, and you have a 95 percent survival rate, that seems like a different road than others go through.

An observant tenant of mine, who happened to notice that I was a long haired blonde on Monday and a shoulder length brunette on Wednesday, inquired, and then shared his story about testicular cancer. His road from diagnosis until *cure* involved a botched surgery, landing him in the hospital for five months and almost killing him. Then once cured from round one of cancer, ten years he later got cancer in the other testicle, which I guess is very uncommon. I wonder if his wife found those lumps.

As I travel here and there, day after day, I am much more observant about cancer clues. A lot of times I can identify a wig, although today's wigs are so great it is hard to tell sometimes. I am also on the lookout for ports and port scars, as well as the telltale bald or scarved heads.

Occasionally, I find myself looking at somebody with extremely short hair and wondering—cancer? Or is that their regular style?

In order to not torture other cancer patients with my story (which I guess I am doing in book form versus approaching someone in the restroom), I occasionally say "Unfortunately, it's not an exclusive club" or "Been there, done that!"

I guess it is clear that I would not have been a very good participant in any support groups. When I was in college at Assumption in Worcester, I was a psychology major for the first two and a half years. As I was taking classes, I realized that I preferred the business management classes over the psychology classes. I could not understand the use of all of that talking, especially if a glass of wine was not involved. In the middle of junior year I changed majors when I realized that my entire philosophy for counseling was "suck it up and deal with it," or "if you don't like it change it," or "stop making excuses."

It does not take a psychologist to realize that I would not be a good psychologist. Empathy is not my greatest strength. As a side note, I am glad that I am the one who had to deal with this cancer situation and not my husband, because I am a way better patient than I am a caregiver.

CHAPTER 13

Taxol

So I started with my twelve weeks of Taxol. My husband's Google MD informed him that for some people Taxol was far worse than AC. I guessed we'd have to see...

My first Taxol, Herceptin, and Pertuzamab or placebo (P?) treatment was March 26, 2013. This was an all-day affair. We arrived at MGH at 8:00 A.M. and did not leave the hospital until 5:45 P.M, because there was a lot of observation time between each of the treatments to see if I was going to have a bad reaction. The observation times isolated the drugs, so that if I did have some sort of reaction they would be able to identify the source.

After the usual rigmarole, getting my vitals taken, accessing my port, visiting the doctor, etc. prior to the start of treatment, instead of getting an infusion of Emend, I got a dose of Benadryl.

When this medication was injected into my port line, I went to the moon! All of a sudden I got tingly from my toes to my head, I started babbling, I was as high as a kite and I felt no pain. We had just been talking about marijuana use as it pertained to symptom relief during chemotherapy, and I realized all I really needed was a dose of intravenous Benadryl.

Fortunately, I did not have any reactions to any of the drugs. Aside from the time-consuming nature of chemotherapy, the fact that I got quality time with friends and family made it bearable. My daughter, Justine, was a frequent chemo escort, and my son Doug would stop in during my chemo, as his class schedule permitted, by taking the T in from Bentley University.

On April 16, the day after the very sad Patriot's Day marathon bombings, we headed to MGH. The town was still very much shut down, and as we approached the hospital, we saw many members of the military, armed with automatic weapons, at the entrances and in the lobbies. There were several bombing victims treated and admitted to the hospital. Although the unease that the bombers were somewhere out there was very real, we felt safe with the added security.

Boston is a wonderful city, and what the Marathon Bombers did was heart wrenching. David and I wished there were something we could do to help all of the people affected by this horrific situation. It is scary how warped some people in society are to hurt others. Doug was walking to the marathon finish line after watching the Red Sox game and was a couple of blocks away when he felt the earth shake from the explosions. There are very few people in the Boston area who were not in some way affected or connected to this tragedy.

A few weeks after the bombing I felt the need to update Dr. Younger about my condition so I sent him the following email.

From: Linda Murphy
Sent: Thursday, May 16, 2013 5:42 PM
To: 'jyounger
Subject: new rash ... Linda Murphy (the cookie lady)

Hi Dr. Younger,

Just thought I would let you know I have a new rash on both arms... The right side is worse than the left.

Pictures are attached.

· ·

They are not bothering me but look gross. They do get irritated in warm water.

I have also included a picture of my son who graduated from college last Sunday. I was very concerned when we first met that chemo would interfere with getting there and enjoying the event! Luckily it was squeezed nicely in between weekly chemo!

I never like to miss a fun time.

Let me know if I should do anything about the rash.

My next appointment with you is 5/28

See you then

:)

 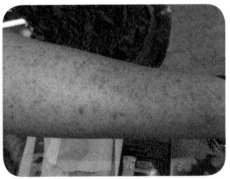

~Linda

How Taxol messed with me while saving my life (hopefully):

- Taxol did not wipe me out like AC but was annoying in other ways.

- Hot flashes and chills...my body couldn't make up its mind. The chills were really weird. They would start in a spot, like the right hip or the left shoulder and burst through my body like an icicle. It made me think about a cartoon. I could see a character being hit by an icicle, and it spreads out and turned the whole person into a chunk of ice. Then a couple minutes later it thawed and I turned into a blazing fire. The hot flashes seemed to be a bit menopause-related—I hadn't had a period since February (three months earlier), so I think the chills were a perk of Taxol. Lucky me!

- During the night the chills would take me by storm, and I would need to attach myself to my husband like an octopus and suck all of his heat from his sleeping body. Then when the chill had passed, I would scoot to my side and remove all of my covers until it cycled again.

- Unfortunately, this cycle would totally interrupt my sleep, sometimes keeping me awake for hours working on temperature control. I was definitely in need of a repair of my broken thermostat.

- I went from 90 percent bald with AC to 99.9999 percent bald with Taxol. At the midway point, I was down to my last few straggly hairs and then to my surprise I started growing some peach fuzz between dose (week) 8 and 9. So officially I had never been 100 percent bald. Take that, Cancer!

- On the annoying front, Taxol ruined my pedicure. Two nails popped off. Really? They weren't painful, they just sort of snubbed their noses at me as they worked their way loose, then popped off at bizarre moments and skittered across the floor. Luckily the nails were brightly painted and easy to find.

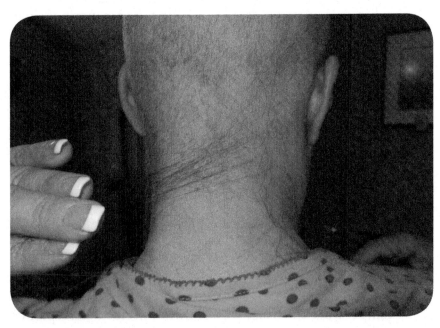

Peach fuzz starting to grow before the last fifty hairs fell out.

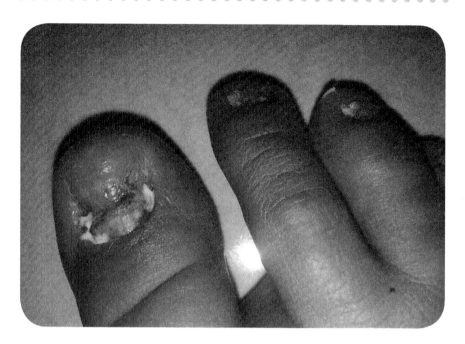

Yuck, my toes were a mess from Taxol!

Things cancer treatments took from me...

- The ability to exercise: something I have bitched and moaned about doing, but when I couldn't...I bitched and moaned about that.

- Neuropathy impeded my piano playing. All right, I admit I really couldn't play very well at all, but it was just one more thing.

- The joy of playing Scramble on my phone while lying in bed; the burn in my hands made it impossible.

- Being proud of my feet: they were a little ugly before, but became totally ugly with missing toenails, not to mention swollen. So ugly fat feet with no toenails—totally disgusting.

- My get up and go—it got up and went. I truly missed my spunk and energy. I was the energizer rabbit but I became more like molasses.

- Three quarters of my wardrobe: Because I had gained so much weight, I could only wear elastic waist skirts that didn't need to harness my thighs. I refused to buy new clothes because I *would* get back on track and lose that cancer weight. (Very different mentality than losing baby weight; Instead of looking at a cute bundle of joy who is sucking out copious calories in the form of breast milk. Now I was scarred, bald and tired, and I couldn't exercise.)

- Driving with my convertible roof down: chemo and radiation and sunshine weren't a good combination.

- Unfortunately, I also had to put my Italian roots on hold and forgo my garden in the summer of 2013 because of lack of time and too much neuropathy.

In mid-April my father and his girlfriend, Marilyn, brought me in for my Taxol infusion. I was very anxious to have my father come in for a chemo treatment so that he could see what it actually was like. It is my opinion that not knowing how bad chemo is can be worse than reality. I think it was good for my dad to see me comfortable, in a private room, having drinks and snacks with great care from Lorraine. For me, there was no pain involved or reactions from the chemotherapy, so I wanted my dad to see that to take the mystery out of such a scary situation.

The next week my husband, David, and my brother, Dave, came in with me, bringing cake pops for the nursing staff made by Dave's girlfriend, Michele. Yes, sorry to confuse you, but my husband, brother, son and father are all named David.

Lorraine was off at a tropical location celebrating her birthday, and so George took charge of my care. George is a very fun guy who was a great substitute for me in Lorraine's absence. He is very caring and you can tell he loves what he does. I was in

good hands for the infusion, and the afternoon went quickly, chatting with my brother with my heart wineglass (filled with ginger ale) my chair/cheerful/cheerleading teddy bear, prayer shawl, and family picture blanket.

David and I have continually said we should make the most of our visits to Boston since we were in the city anyway. We tried to do this at least a couple of times. After one infusion, when Heidi W and Adrianne joined me, we had Heidi drop us off at Faneuil Hall for some walking and dinner. It was a beautiful night, and we had a nice time taking in the sights. Boston really is a great city.

One would think that with all of the negative side effects of Taxol, I would be glad to skip one. Oddly enough, I wasn't. On Sunday, May 19, my neuropathy was so bad that changing the beds had me in tears; my hands were so tingly and painful. My husband caught me during this rare brief breakdown and insisted that I tell the doctor what was happening.

We were warned by Lorraine that we should definitely tell the doctor if the neuropathy was bad, because if you push the envelope and cross the line, you can end up with permanent nerve damage. To be cured of cancer and then live with pain for the rest of your life, which would prevent me from long walks and other activities seemed like a bad idea. The concept

Adrianne and Heidi W. two longtime friends who clocked many, many hours with me in the infusion unit. Both brought puzzles and games to help pass the time.

of permanent impairment convinced me to e-mail the doctor about the situation.

At my doctor's appointment before my scheduled Taxol treatment, I met with Maria, who was just back from maternity leave after having an adorable baby boy she named Hunter. She is a really sweet person. Oddly, having met Maria prior to her going on her four-month leave, then she returned and I was still in treatment, made me realize how stinkin' long I had been doing this!

May 21— Maria and Dr. Younger met with David and me and collectively decided to skip Taxol. I felt like I failed. I couldn't stay healthy enough to get everything I was supposed to. Neuropathy is really tough to describe and rate. It isn't like putting something on the 1–10 pain scale. It varied throughout the day and was more of a sensation than a degree of pain. Reluctantly, we went home, hoping that missing this treatment wouldn't be an issue.

Over the course of my week off, I admitted that skipping the treatment was the right call. The symptoms remained present throughout the week and didn't show signs of subsiding until the following weekend.

Linda with Nurse Extraordinaire, Lorraine,
Skyping Mom Murphy

The next week I was feeling well enough to get the whole enchilada—Taxol, Herceptin, and P?. As per protocol, the Taxol dose was reduced by 20 percent to try to avoid further side effects. Because of the trial and various protocols, every time Taxol was skipped it must be reduced, and because of the P? study, this could only be done one time.

On June 4, I had a Taxol treatment. This was what we termed a "short day," with a blood draw through the port, a quick doctor's appointment, and just Taxol. Lorraine took wonderful care of me as usual. During such an involved infusion schedule, which lasted over a year I got to know my medical team quite well. Her daughter got married near the beginning of my treatments and by then was expecting a baby. Very exciting news; it was fun to share in these lives. As I have marched progressively up in weight, Lorraine has been losing. She has been an iron woman, having the willpower to pass on the cookies. In order to give her some treats, we would get her an unsweetened ice tea with three lemons to let her know we loved and appreciated her. Also, during my treatments, she joined me in Skype conversations with my mother-in-law, who lived in North Carolina.

Once again, June 11, I had to tell the troops that my neuropathy was pretty bad. Dr. Younger was off to Scotland on a much-deserved vacation, so I was booked with Dr. Shin and

Maria for my pre-Taxol appointment. Honestly, I didn't realize how dependent I had become on Dr. Younger and felt a little lost without him.

Dr. Shin and Maria both examined me and assessed my situation through a series of questions. They determined that my neuropathy was right on the cusp of causing me serious permanent nerve damage. Having already missed one dose, I felt that I really needed to continue and get my treatments. After the assessment, they determined that my treatment would be cancelled.

This was supposed to be my eleventh treatment. Because I was missing this treatment, and I had skipped one before—that was it, the end, no more Taxol because of the standards for that drug administration. *Shock*! Really, no more? But they said *twelve*, not ten... Did this mean that they didn't kill it all? Is there still some cancer? I needed chemo. What if skipping these last two Taxol infusions meant that the feisty cancer cells weren't all gone and I would die...

Dr. Shin looked at me and said, "You look concerned." Well, that did it. The flood gates opened. After all these months of stoically smiling though every appointment, I lost it. Dr. Shin was just too compassionate, and it broke down my wall of valor!

We left the hospital dumbfounded and in a daze. The Taxol, which was kicking the sh#@ out of me, was over. I realized that the risk of permanent damage would be horrible, but having cancer kill me would suck even more. I was unable to believe I was finished.

As David and I were driving out of the city it dawned on me...I could resume my drinking. Yeah! It had been one week since my last treatment, and that was my own predetermined alcohol consumption policy. One week after my last Taxol, I would start drinking again and now, premature as it was, let the party begin! On my ride home, I texted a couple of friends who I knew would want to help me jump off the wagon and then sent an e-mail to more people to have them join in the fun.

From: Linda Murphy
Sent: Tuesday, June 11, 2013 4:46 PM
To: my wonderful friends
Subject: a real party

I am filled with mixed emotions as I was turned away from chemo today because the neuropathy in my fingers and toes is pretty bad, and they are afraid it will be permanent if I had Taxol today... (A risk versus return decision)

And because I missed today...I am done.

I have been very emotional about it. I can't believe it is time to start healing and am nervous that I had only ten of the scheduled twelve Taxols.

I will still need to have two types of chemos every three weeks until March 2014, but they are considered different and not so abusive to the rest of my body.

So tonight, my friend, Maria R, who gave up alcohol with me as an act of solidarity, (Something none of you other lushes did!!!) and I will jump off the wagon together at Funky Murphy's in Worcester at 7:00 p.m.

My husband has agreed to be our designated driver to and from Boylston.

Let me know if you can join us.

So far Susan M, Linda B, Michelle, Laurie L, and Maria are going.

A few of you have been frequent chemo party attendees... hope you can come to the fun party serving cosmos instead of battery acid!

Adrianne is in Amsterdam, and Susan E is on the Cape... They will be missed! Anne and Sharon...Texas is a bit far! :(

No pressure...I know it is a week night and quite a drive for some of you.

David will send out an update with the gory details soon but wanted to include you in the good stuff if you are able to join me!

You have all been sooooo amazing!

I am so lucky to have all of you in my life!

XOXO

(Meghan, although I didn't have chemo your cookies went to good use with the radiologist and oncologist I saw today)

:)

~Linda

Michelle, me, Maria R, Laurie, Susan M, and Linda B celebrating the end of Taxol at Funky Murphy's in Worcester

On June 18, I had a Herceptin Pertuzumab/Placebo treatment. My dad and Marilyn once again brought me in for the fun this particular day. We started off with a blood draw done by Lorraine through my port. Then we met with Dr. Shin again. I asked her to please refrain from being so empathetic. I didn't like to cry because it loosened my fake eyelashes. Once again, she was the sweetest ever.

She spoke of the next steps: radiation, H/P?, and Tamoxifen. This reminded me of the long road that was still to come. She also spoke about an after-the-cancer support group. I can definitely understand how a person can go from all of this undivided attention, especially from medium and heavy cancer to being *done*. I was getting tractor trailers full of care, love, and attention. I got cards, presents, calls, texts, cookies, and medical attention on almost a daily basis. When I transitioned to, hopefully, survivor, I would have to get my attention by sharing my story with strangers I encountered on the street who looked like they had cancer. After all, I know how much I have enjoyed hearing endless cancer stories, *not*!

During one of my infusions, my brother, Mike, and his children also stopped in. I was not surprised. I had made chemo sound like so much fun everyone wanted to come. Free ice cream is a real draw. When I heard that my niece and nephew were going to stop in (I make it sound easy, but it was a forty minute ride for them to come to Boston), I never delivered cookies to the chemo nurses but kept them for the kids—oops.

On my way home from what I term the easier chemos, supposedly with no side effects, my right arm and hand went a bit haywire. It started tingling and pulsing. My hand felt like it was on fire. If I hadn't just had H/P? I would have thought it was a heart attack (except that it was my right arm and not my left). Since the last Taxol was June 4, my neuropathy was getting much better. This infusion stirred it all up again and now I was back to pain, tingling, and swelling. At least I had three weeks until my next infusion, which should be plenty of time to recover.

CHAPTER 14

Next Step, Radiation!

Cookies in hand, on June 11, 2013, my husband and I weaved through the innards of MGH to find the radiation area. Although brightly lit and decorated, we were sixty feet down below the city of Boston, three stories below street level. Meeting with Dr. Taghian, my wonderful radiologist, was pretty uneventful. During our first visit to Massachusetts General Hospital back in November, Dr. Taghian was available to see us, and although it was miles and miles away, told us all the gory details we had to look forward to after the surgeries and chemo.

Needless to say this time it was more serious. We reviewed the multitude of side effects and problems that can occur from radiation. Even the fact that radiation, like chemo, can give you cancer—how reassuring. So the way we heard it, the risks of heart damage were great, especially, when you add it to the heart-damaging Herceptin and P? I was already getting. And lucky me, because of some stray factor I would also have my neck area radiated. The fun was really just going on and on. After careful review, I signed my life away and was told to return for heart position mapping in a couple of weeks.

Luckily, I happened to have tickets from my dad to the Red Sox game on June 27, the night before mapping. My daughter, Justine, and I headed into Boston for an overnight stay and watched a great game against the Blue Jays. The Sox had a nice 7–5 win which was fun all the way around. We found an over-eighteen club, Jillian's, and Justine and I worked to master the video beer pong game. Much less messy than real beer pong and lots of fun. After a photo shoot in the photo booth we went back to our room. The next morning we headed over to MGH for our eleven o'clock appointment. I was told we would meet with Dr. Taghian first, to sign some paper work. When he arrived and started to review the forms, I told him we had already done this two weeks ago. With the stream of patients he sees (how sad that this club has so many members), he really didn't remember. When I explained that I came with my husband and brought cookies, it came back to him. Those cookies really did pay off.

I requested at the beginning of the mapping appointment for Justine to be able to watch the happenings, since she was entering nursing school in the fall. They were happy to oblige. After donning my johnny we entered a room with a very interesting contraption. It reminded me of a gynecologists chair and gave me pause as to what kind of torture was going to be inflicted upon me there. Luckily, the stirrups were for my arms and not my legs, but it still wasn't a lot of fun.

Stretched out with my arms above my head, the radiation team got to work. The nice man, young enough to be my son, exposed my breast and then outlined the breast fat with a fancy metal kind of tape to define what remained of my still-oversized left boob. He then proceeded to take a series of porno shots of my voluptuous bosom. I was a little disturbed by this. I explained to the nice man that if I knew I was having a naked photo shoot, I would have worn my blonde wig. He didn't get it, but my daughter and I had a good laugh.

They took pictures, I think a CAT scan; I breathed, I held

my breath, and breathed some more. Justine was in the booth and got to see where my heart was positioned in my chest and how a consistent deep breath moved my ribs and chest wall out away from my heart. This deep-breath method is something that MGH radiologists use to prevent damage to the heart. The first five weeks of radiation would involve the entire breast, and then one to two weeks just a concentration of the area where I had cancer. During the concentrated dose, they would shoot the rays at the area where I had the tumor through a dense stone that some mathematicians/physicists used fancy calculus equations to figure out. One thing I didn't understand was how we had been taught so much about covering up our bodies before we get a little radiation from an X-ray, but in here they are zapping me with intense radiation, in a lead-lined room, and this was supposed to cure me. We ended the session with some fancy body art as they tattooed marks on me for proper alignment during radiation. In my mind tattoos are an integral part of being a cool motorcycle mama so follow along as I once again digress.

Long ago, my husband begged, pleaded, and used manipulation to try and convince me that he should be "allowed" to get a motorcycle. I have always been petrified about motorcycles because of the risk of injury. We had school-age kids, and I really didn't want to spend my time between mothering my children and caring for my paraplegic husband if he crashed. Also, the thought of one of the kids getting on the back of the bike really scared me.

Even though I was totally against motorcycles, my philosophy as a wife is that I try not to say "no" to what the second wife will say "yes" to. So I agreed to "let" David get a motorcycle if he agreed that he would have to ride alone until our last baby went off to college. At that point, many years ago, I agreed to get on it when we were finally empty nesters.

My job is in real estate management. We have some one-bedroom apartments, and this size apartment is a popular first stop for the newly divorced man. They move in and, within minutes, buy a Harley and shortly thereafter the tall blonde with the killer body shows up and they ride off to Laconia, New Hampshire for the weekend. After seeing this pattern way too many times, I agreed to the bike, even though I will never be tall or very thin. But thanks to my wigs, I was blonde. So, unintentionally, I was as ready as I would ever be now that, compliments of MGH radiology department, I am officially tattooed! That's right, I had five badass tats on my chest, and I was ready to ride!

Now, with the purchase of some black pleather pants I was some happening babe. LOL!

***Baby graduated from high school, five new tats
and I am now a biker chick!***

Also, for the record, one of the cookie brigade baked cookies for the CAT scan techs, and they really appreciated it. The cookies, again and again, made a day that was routine a little bit more special and I think my care a little better.

Fourth of July weekend, I had a couple of cancer encounters. At the post office, I was discussing getting stamps and wanted to be sure that I wasn't paying extra for any of them, like breast cancer stamps. I was assured I was only paying the going rate without any upcharge. The woman behind me ordered two sheets of breast cancer stamps with the charity upcharge attached, I felt a bit cheap and felt the need to state, "Now I feel bad. I actually have cancer right now and won't pay the upcharge." and left the building.

The woman followed me out and told me about her own course of treatment for breast cancer including most of the fun that I had. The real kicker was that she got a cancer from the radiation. She developed a rash in the radiated area and had to have a mastectomy on the breast she had the lumpectomy on and more chemo. UGH! She encouraged me to be sure that the radiation was necessary before I had it but did say it only happens in a hundred people per year, ever, or something like that. I am not good with those statistics.

The other cancer encounter was at BJ's wholesale club. I was checking out, and the woman cashier at the next lane caught my attention to ask me if I just got my hair done because it looked so amazing. I told her it was a wig, and she could have this hair too. This also happened when I was checking out at a hotel and also another grocery store. My Miranda wig gets way more attention and compliments than my real hair ever did; maybe I will go blonde.

Oh no, here we go again. Three weeks passed, and my neuropathy was as bad as ever. Supposedly Herceptin does not cause neuropathy, but my husband found an article using his new medical doctor degree from Google, suggesting that

Pertuzumab can cause neuropathy. The good news: perhaps I was getting Pertuzumab instead of the placebo; the bad news: it was giving me neuropathy. So on July 9, cookies in hand, thanks to one of my favorite bakers (Heidi M, who baked more than her fair share and always did an amazing assortment and presentation), my friend Anne and her daughter, Bree, visiting from Texas, and I headed to Boston. Instead of just heading to infusion as scheduled, we were squeezed in for a visit with Dr. Younger and Karleen, a nurse in charge of the Pertuzumab study. He was just back from a fabulous, well-deserved vacation in Scotland. They agreed my right hand looked swollen and darker in color, as well as both of my feet.

Apparently neuropathy is supposed to be symmetrical. Because I pride myself on being different, mine was not, so this gave them concern that I may have a blood clot. If it were on the cancer-boob side, they would think lymphedema, but because it was port side, they think blood clot. Off we went to hematology to talk to them and get their opinion on the possibility of a blood clot. When I arrived, I was greeted by the beautiful perky blonde who I thought was too young to put in my port. After examining me, she agreed with Dr. Younger's thoughts that an ultrasound of my arm and port area was warranted. Anne and I had a seven year old with us, and though I thought she could watch TV in our room while they pumped me full of Dr. Slamon's secret recipe, instead we just dragged her all over the hospital. Luckily we got a one o'clock ultrasound appointment back in the same building where we started, Yawkey, and headed right over.

Roy took me in at about 1:10 pm and slathered me with KY jelly—hey, don't get the wrong idea—it was just for the test. He used his magic wand and checked the plumbing for clogs. I wished Justine had gotten to see this test. It was really neat the way he could look at the arteries (or veins, or both, I forget), both from a bird's eye view of long strips and as a cross section looking straight down the pipes. As he looked down the pipes, he would press down to see if the vessel would compress. If it flattened out there was no blood clot, but if it didn't that meant there was.

Luckily, every one squished nicely so there was no blood clot to deal with. The technician of this particular test was permitted to give the results to the patient immediately, since leaving the hospital with a blood clot can kill you. No blood clot. Instead of returning to the hematology department, I went back up a few floors to see Dr. Younger again. All was well. He suggested that I go home and let him know how I was doing in a couple of weeks.

So cycle 5 of the H/P? was cancelled. According to Dr. Younger, the neuropathy did indicate that I might be getting

CHAPTER 15

Thirty Radiation Treatments, Oh My!

So I began radiation as I had tackled this entire situation. Head on. As Larry the Cable Guy would say "Git 'er done," and that's just what I intended to do. On Monday morning, July 22, I headed in to Boston on the earlier side, because they needed to do a trial run before my first treatment with my team at eleven o'clock. I was not sure what the purpose of that appointment was, but they did some more X-rays and added a sixth tattoo to my already tatted-up torso. Luckily, Dr. Taghian told me from the beginning that Massachusetts law required that insurance companies pay to have radiation tattoos removed after treatment. It was a nice gesture, and I would probably take them up on it when I was done with all of this nonsense.

After an appointment for the trial run, the tests, X-rays, and scans were passed on to the physicists, the math whizzes, who do these very involved problems in order to avoid damaging my heart while trying to cure me. In between my appointments, my friend Michelle's daughter, Hilary, who was in Boston visiting a friend, came and joined me for a cup of coffee. I had so much fabulous quality time with people because of this illness. It really made the whole situation almost fun. You probably can't believe I said that; it is so totally inappropriate. As my husband said about my mother-in-law and me, we would have "a ball at a bull castration," and I guess this was no different with the way I go about my life.

After a delightful coffee out on the Mass General patio in the glorious sunshine, I head sixty feet below the ground to the LL3 in the Lunder building. Meeting the ladies who would be my radiation team went well. They are pretty and peppy, just the way I like people I need to see frequently. The four to five person team varied slightly day to day. The ladies worked a four-day ten-hour day weekly schedule, so they were each off one day per week. Because I have no shortage of the gift of gab, I learned a lot about the technicians and got a glimpse into their lives over the course of treatment.

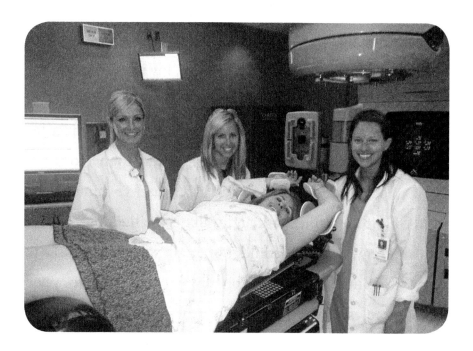

Cassie, Helen, Jill, Liz, Colleen, and Kerrie were my regulars, with a smattering of others over the thirty treatments. As I was talking about my son David one day and explaining that he was single, I realized that it would be a good chance to set him up with Cassie. Through all of the tools of modern technology, they connected. I think they went out a couple of times and had some fun, but that was all as Cupid didn't hit his mark. Apparently, my work as an overinvolved, meddling, matchmaking mother did not pan out. I was really hoping that they would fall madly in love and get married. There are a few reasons this would be amazing: first of all, it would be great in this book. Secondly, it would have been a clear sign that this disease would have a true purpose, and good could come out of it. I must admit, if that had worked out, my whole perspective on the events of the past year really would have been altered. It would be the ultimate silver lining. And last, it would make my son happy, and that is always a mother's dream for her kids.

Six weeks, Monday through Friday, a forty-five-minute drive to MGH, if no traffic, park and walk in the building, change into a johnny, wait, sometimes not at all, sometimes thirty to forty-five minutes, depending on any emergencies, get zapped for six minutes between lining my tattoos up and repositioning me as needed. Change back into my clothes, back to the garage, and forty-five minutes home. So basically, because I chose to do all of my treatments at Massachusetts General Hospital, my daily commitment was three hours. I was braced for a long arduous month and a half.

A friend of mine who had cancer lite, lumpectomy, and radiation, had a great idea. Before starting treatment she blew up thirty balloons and every day when she got home she popped one as a visual barometer of how much progress she had made. What a great idea! Although I learned about it too late to use this motivational aide, it seems like a great idea to pass along.

On one of the first days of radiation, Justine acted as my chauffeur. We went through the regular rigmarole of parking and then headed in. I changed while she waited. It was a very quiet day, and there was only one other person in the waiting room.

When we were back in the car, Justine told me that when I went into the treatment room for my zapping, this other person, a middle-aged man, struck up a conversation with Justine that went something like this:

"Is that your mom?"

"Don't expect her to look that happy and chipper for too much longer. Radiation really does a number on you. You can expect your mom to start vomiting, be so tired she can't even lift her head, lose tons of weight, and feel really horrible."

This goes against everything that I had told Justine radiation was going to be. This guy really scared her.

His wife and I reentered the waiting room from our treatment rooms about the same time. I think before cancer she and I were about the same age, and now she looked like she was about ninety years old. She was walking hunched over holding her stomach, she had shoulder-length very thin gray frizzy hair, her teeth were all dark and crooked, and she was down to skin and bones.

When Justine told me what the guy said, I was furious. How could this guy scare my daughter like this? It had to be clear that he was talking to a young woman whose mother was going through a life-threatening illness. His need to talk about his plight was misguided. I really wanted to tell him how inappropriate it was to have said this to Justine.

I found out later that the woman was being treated for stomach cancer and probably was not going to make it. I put my anger aside and chose not to tell this guy off for being so insensitive. He was going through too much on his own, and maybe being able to talk about it to Justine lightened his burden a little.

I must admit the time flew by over the course of the six weeks. After the hell of chemotherapy, radiation was a walk in the park. During the radiation, I continued on my every-three-week Herceptin/P(?) schedule.

Every Tuesday, over the six weeks of treatment, I had an appointment with Dr. Taghian. Honestly, he got as excited about the cookies as Dr. Younger did. I think the nurses who you see for a longer period of time and have a more intimate relationship with get spoiled more frequently than the doctors.

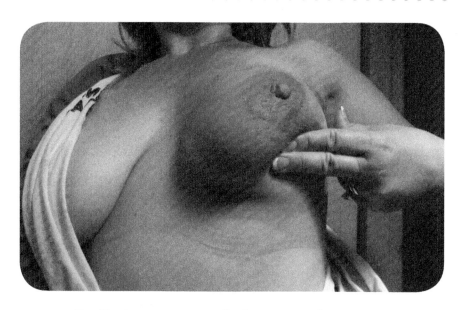

Radiation—tanning bed on steroids! OUCH!

During one of these appointments towards the beginning of treatment Dr. Taghian explained to me that I needed to put cream on my treated breast and neck area three times a day following radiation. This helped the skin so it did not break down.

At one of these appointments, David, following a continual theme that he had, which was "what assurance can you give me that my wife is going to be fine," entered into a discussion with Dr. Taghian about the impact that positive attitude had on treatment and recovery. It was the doctor's opinion that patients who came in optimistic and uplifted had much more successful outcomes than people who were moping and depressed throughout the situation. It was interesting to hear a medical professional say that you can influence the success of your cancer treatments through a positive attitude. Quite frankly, I had sort of used that as a running joke every time someone said that I would be fine because of my positive attitude.

There were quite a few times that I used radiation as a springboard toward other fun activities. On some days, friends or family would come in for the ride and wait with me through my treatment and follow it up with time in Boston, a shopping spree, or maybe just lunch.

All of my appointments for radiation were scheduled for eleven o'clock. This gave me the ability to avoid the morning rush and get out of Boston before the afternoon traffic jam.

About once a week I would drive from my radiation appointment in Boston up to Cambridge to take David Jr. out for lunch on my way home. A couple of nights my husband and I stayed in Boston at a waterfront hotel where we would enjoy walking around the city (as much as I could between my neuropathy and my hip), a dinner in the north end, or Faneuil Hall, or sometimes even a stroll down Newbury Street. Then we'd circle back to Massachusetts General Hospital at eleven the next morning.

In search of some relief, I decided I would give acupuncture a try and see if that would help with the swelling in my right arm, as well as the neuropathy. I figure if something has been around

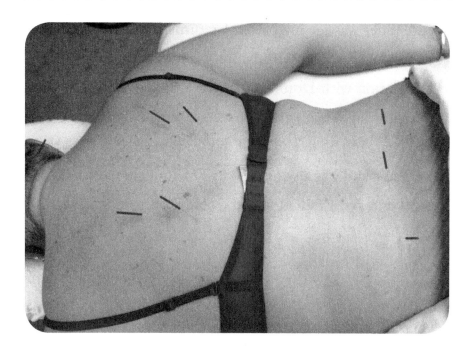

for thousands and thousands of years, there has to be some good that can come out of it. I went for a few sessions with Tamara Allen in Westborough. She was very professional and although I cannot say for sure whether or not this helped my situation, I was feeling better. It is my impression that it did lessen my neuropathy and help reduce some of the swelling. It seems like acupuncture helps the flow of your lymphatic system and your nervous system for all around better health and well-being.

A nurse told me she used acupuncture to help with infertility, and although she cannot say if it directly cured her problem, she ended up having a beautiful baby.

In the spring of 2014, after I had finished treatments and

my shoulder was feeling better, I returned for more acupuncture. I combined that with lymphatic massage and scar tissue manipulation with Donna, at the Health and Wellness group in Westborough, in an effort to reduce the size and swelling of my still gargantuan left breast. I did see some results from these treatments, and was also assured by Dr. Younger that the swelling was due to the radiation and would eventually subside.

CHAPTER 16

Bullshit from the Balcony

I understand that my pastor isn't God, but sometimes I wonder how he reads my mind. Sometimes, when I am having an internal struggle, whether I am mad at someone, or I have done something unkind, I can't figure out how to make it right. My minister chooses that week to smack me upside the head with a sermon that drives the solution home. The reason this is so weird is because I never usually discuss this with anyone. When I am on a moral balance beam, I do pray about it and debate about it internally in hopes of finding the best outcome. I guess I should be grateful that my spiritual leader comes to the rescue with words of wisdom to guide me.

As I headed through this maze of cancer, I must admit I was having difficulty with God. Really? As the old adage goes, "Why me?" In my opinion, I am a good person, I try really hard to be kind and nice to everyone, I try to be a good Christian. I go to church regularly. I pray. So why have I been given cancer? People are so well meaning. They tell me God will see me through. If prayers cure cancer, I actually could skip chemo, because I was on every prayer chain in every church of every person I know. It gave me a good feeling to know that so many people were praying intensely for my full recovery. Yet the question still needs an answer. Why me?

One of David's tenants sent me a little sheet of fabric with writing on it that I was instructed to insert between my pillow and my pillowcase and sleep on every night. It contained prayers that were going to heal me while I slept. Sounded like a good idea to me. They told David it worked for someone else they knew who had cancer and got healed. I immediately brought it upstairs and tucked it in between my pillow and pillowcase. Although I was having my doubts about religion, I would try anything.

I met my cousin for lunch for her birthday at the beginning of my radiation. In addition to being cousins, we are lifelong friends. After we covered all of the usual catch-up topics, I broached the topic of my doubts about my faith. Her reply caught me by surprise. I wasn't aware that she was now a believer of past lives. So her answer was that in my prior life, I had needs that weren't met. Apparently, my need to know I am loved and a need for extra attention are things I was deprived of in my past lives, so that need is being met in my present life through my cancer saga. This was a lot to digest. I would have to think more about this at a later time.

Then, the following Sunday, my minister, who was dealing with the personal struggle of having a sick grandchild, broached the topic. First, he said, when asked the question of why bad things happen and what to say in answer to that question posed by loved ones—the answer is, "I don't know." Then when reaching for the Biblical explanation, he explained that there was a greater reason. He used the analogy that the rains need to come before you can harvest a crop. He of course used Bible verses to prove this point. As I sat in my corner of the balcony with the videographer, I had to quell the very urgent need to shout from my perch, "Bullshit!"

Jesus and God are supposed to be loving and compassionate,

so I don't get it. It is assumed that the love God has for me is infinity times infinity more than I love my children. I would do anything to protect my sons and daughter from harm.

It is understandable, and I can appreciate that people who have no control of the outcome for my cancer, want to make me feel that I will be fine. So I have heard many times that I will be fine. Everyone was praying for my full recovery. God wouldn't give me anything I can't handle. God is good. Thank God they caught it early. Thank God…

My true feeling about God is that we can't just *thank* him for the good and not *blame* him for the bad. It is unclear to me why I should thank God that they caught my cancer early, but I can't blame God that I got cancer at all.

Our church has a written prayer list on the back of the weekly order of service. I put two uncles on this list, because they both had cancer. They both died on the younger side because of the disease. After letting my spiritual leader know about my cancer, I was very clear that I did not want my name on this list. To me this list did not worked as intended, and I didn't want to end up like my uncles.

Another friend, who has a renewed faith, commonly termed a "born-again" Christian, had a unique story to share. She had a friend who looked at having cancer in a different way. If she was cured and lived she won and got to be with her family and friends here on earth for much longer. If she died, then she got to go to heaven and meet Jesus, and that was also a win. I wish my faith were strong enough to feel this way.

My emotions swung in many directions. Sometimes I thought I would beat this thing, and sometimes I thought that it was going to take my life, and I'd be leaving my family and friends prematurely. Hopefully, there is a heaven. It would be really amazing, if when I die, there is a white light at the end of a tunnel, and my grandmother is there to greet me with her loving smile and pull me into a long-missed embrace. On the other hand, if there is no God and no heaven, then that would leave nothing. So when I eventually pass away, as is inevitable for all of us, and if there is nothing, then...nothing. I won't be disappointed, because I just won't *be*.

As I stated before, a person's priest or pastor is not God. When I was diagnosed in November, I stopped by my pastor's office after service and told him about my diagnosis. I was a little disappointed that over the course of my year and a half of treatment, unless I reached out to him by stopping to say hello after service, we had no communication. I am not sure exactly what I expected, but I was hoping for more spiritual support during this difficult time, especially given my uncertainties. The ladies in the church who knew about my diagnosis were very supportive, and one deacon in particular would continually send me cards on the days I needed them most. She said she sent cards when the spirit moved her. Hmmmm...

CHAPTER 17

The Silver Lining

Although it is said that "everything happens for a reason," it is hard for me to believe this. Many years ago, I said this to my son Doug, and he replied, "Tell me one reason a child would have cancer." He has always been wise beyond his years. This one response has prevented me from ever saying that lame phrase again.

That being said, I found the silver lining in any and every way I could in this situation.

The most evident bonus I received from this health crisis was seeing my husband's strength, love, and support. A health crisis can either make a marriage stronger or tear it apart. Making my marriage stronger was a definite plus. I have a friend who was not as fortunate, and her health crisis ended the marriage. Of course, I'm sure it was not the health crisis alone, but a stressor like this on a marriage can be the straw that breaks the camel's back.

Living just forty-five minutes outside of Boston, one would think that we would take advantage of all of the fabulous activities available to us. Prior to cancer, that had not been the case. Making the most out of a bad situation, we used our frequent expeditions to Boston to make the most of the city. Over the course of the year and a half traipsing to and from Boston, I enjoyed a few overnights, dinner in town with friends, Duck Tours, Newbury Street, Red Sox games, a Rihanna concert (the one where she was three hours late coming onstage), a Rick Springsteen tribute band, and also a fun night watching Elton John with friends

Hopefully, I would never need this skill again, but I also learned how to wear fake eyelashes and paint on eyebrows.

One of my favorite silver linings was my new friend, Jill. One day, when I was getting my nails done by Kevin, the other manicurists kept using my name. Hi, Linda! How are you, Linda! I

Elton John concert after my dewigging appointment,
November 12, 2013. Heidi W, Michelle, Jill, me,
Nancy, Ali, and Justine.

found this to be extremely strange, since they spent more time speaking to each other in Vietnamese than saying my name. What they were trying to do was let Jill, another client, who was getting her nails done a couple seats over to realize that I was the person they had told her about.

It turned out that Jill had been diagnosed with breast cancer in February 2013, a few months after I had been. She had already had a double mastectomy and was scheduled to start chemo the next day. Jill and I hit it off. Apparently, our nail technicians had decided to play cancer matchmakers and fixed us up. They did a great job, and although I am not a support group kind of girl, it was really wonderful to have somebody to talk to about the various phases of treatment. Although she was diagnosed much later than me, I was only about two months ahead of her for treatments, but because of her kind of cancer versus my HER2+, she would be finished with all of her treatments long before me.

Quality time with my family and friends during this detour of life has been amazing. It is a situation like cancer that truly shows you who cares about you, who doesn't care about you, and everything in between. I do understand that people have different ways of coping, and for some people this situation was very uncomfortable. On the big scale, I was very impressed with the love and support I got from so many people. However, not to be greedy, but certain people did disappoint me with their lack of contact and concern. It really does help you understand relationships in a way like no other. On the other hand, there were friends of mine who rose to new heights in my eyes, as they went above and beyond, over and over again, to give of themselves, to check in on me, or give up hours of time to be by my side.

I don't think a lot of people would look at things the way I do, but I have frequently said to my husband that I love when people show their true colors, so that you actually know the intentions of their heart and where you stand with them. In this situation, people truly showed their colors, mostly in a good way, but some people I expected more from were absent.

CHAPTER 18

The Road to Recovery

Ugh! Up thirty pounds (really it was 37.5 pounds but I was in a little bit of denial about how bad it really was). There were a few reasons I got so fat. Obviously, I put way too much food in my mouth for various reasons. One of the reasons I ate so much is because a large ice cream, a high-fat cheesy spinach artichoke dip, and a bag of chips does make you feel better than a bowl of leafy greens with low-fat dressing. I really wish I didn't eat with sadness and stress, but the bottom line is I do and it does feel good!

Some of the other reasons I got fat were the medications. I have always thought these were really lame excuses for gaining weight because you need to put food in your mouth to get fat, but between the bad start with Danazol, which boosted me up nine pounds as I was eating like a truck driver, then steroids as part of my chemo regimen, I was off to a running start towards gaining weight.

During our chemo class with Lorraine, she said that breast cancer treatments make you gain weight. I really thought that was a little crazy, as I always believed that cancer and chemo made you skinny. But, sadly, she was correct. The chemotherapies for women with estrogen- and progesterone-positive tumors strip your body of these hormones, forcing you into menopause and sending you into a bit of a tailspin as far weight gain goes.

As a side note, when I was talking to Dr. Younger about my type of tumor, the ER/PR positive type, I knew that my tumor was a hormone pig, and I shared with him how I thought the therapies worked. I thought he piggybacked the chemo on to the hormones, gave me some extra, and when the tumor ate the hormones, it also ate the chemo/poison, and that is what killed it.

This, by the way, is 100 percent incorrect and not how it works. If I understood his explanation correctly, it is that the treatment stripped my body of all of the hormones to starve the tumor, while killing every fast-growing cell in my body; assuming the tumor was a fast-growing cell, it would also be annihilated. Once again, my disclaimer is that I have no clue what I'm talking about. If you want the facts, please read a different book.

So I am fat, bald, toenail-less, burned from radiation, and scarred. How lovely!

Contrary to everyone's words of encouragement, the weight was not just falling off. The last harsh Taxol was June 4, 2013. I admit that the summer was lost to radiation and neuropathy. Therefore, no effort was made on my part to move forward on the road to recovery.

On August 30, 2013, I had my last radiation treatment. After dedicating three-plus hours a day over the course of six weeks, the reward and finale was that you get to ring a bell. When I spoke to Dr. Taghian, I told him I thought this was totally lame. I thought champagne and lobster would be a more appropriate ending to such an arduous, draining, and damaging series of treatments.

Nonetheless, the day of my last treatment, my radiation technicians, my husband, and my friend Laurie (who brought me flowers to celebrate), stood by as I walked over and rang the bell. I cried. How ridiculous! At the end of each of these intense cycles of treatment the letdown is extreme. Because you work so hard to keep up a positive attitude, put on a brave face, and power through, when you realize you do not need to prop yourself up to that degree any longer, you tend to just melt.

Two days later, on the following Sunday, we dropped Doug off at Bentley University and then on Monday we moved Justine into Regis College. So on Labor Day 2013, we became empty nesters and also could see that the worst part of my treatments were over.

We celebrated our newfound freedom with an all-you-can-eat Chinese food buffet. My absolute favorite food, crab rangoons, along with white zinfandel, and I was well on my way to a new focus and determination to get myself back to normal.

Tuesday morning I got up, put on my exercise clothes, and headed to the treadmill. UGH! It is amazing how quickly your muscles and stamina wane. Just six months prior, while getting A/C treatments, I was able to keep up the majority of my exercise regime. Now I could barely walk on the treadmill.

Part of my plan for getting myself back in shape was what I personally called the "Trophy Wife Diet." For the record, David took exception to the name that I gave this diet, because he felt it made him look shallow. I named the diet this, because I wanted to look like a trophy wife for myself, not necessarily because David needed one.

The components of the Trophy Wife Diet were as follows. First thing I gave up was all soda. I was only drinking diet soda but I was told by a doctor friend of mine that when you drink a sweet soda, your brain gets a message from your taste buds that a high-calorie food is entering the body. This causes a release of insulin, which then tells your body to store the incoming calories, because it senses it will be a high-calorie food due to the sweetness. Apparently, different foods entering the body are treated differently. Some are more readily stored as fat, and others are more quickly burned.

Because of this revelation, I also tried to use less artificial sweetener in my coffee and went from two packets to one packet. It took a little while to adjust to the less sweet taste, but now I think my coffee tastes delicious!

The only drawback (if one would consider this a drawback) of giving up soda is I think I drink more wine because of the lack of other options. I do enjoy my white zinfandel. Hot tea and unsweetened ice tea are the other options that I enjoy when I am out and about before two o'clock in the afternoon, because the caffeine would otherwise keep me up all night.

Part of unsweetening myself was to give up all sweets, except for perhaps one bite of birthday cake on a special occasion. My usual diet plan was to have a medium coffee and a Boston cream doughnut, about 280 calories, for lunch, thinking that 280 calories for a doughnut was equal to 280 calories for a sandwich. Apparently that is not the case, and I was sabotaging myself, because the calories that I was bringing into my body were being processed in such a way as to be more than the actual value.

Another large change I made was to give up all of the bread baskets before meals at restaurants and to also cut down on bread and carbs in general, focusing on protein, vegetables, and fruit. At first the bread was taunting me from the wicker basket. But as time went on, I got to the point where it just did not interest me at all. Now, I can even go to Bertucci's and skip the rolls!

As far as alcohol consumption goes, I only drink wine, and I always put ice cubes in it so that it gets diluted and lasts longer. A glass of wine is about 122 calories, and I know how much alcohol I am consuming and can moderate myself better. Occasionally in the past, when I had a mixed drink, it could hit me like a ton of bricks, and all of a sudden I would be quite tipsy without realizing how I'd gotten there so quickly. Another drawback of the mixed drink was the huge amount of calories with all of the juices and syrups.

When I was a child, I was informed on a regular basis that children were starving in Ethiopia, and if I did not eat every bite of food on my plate, somehow they would be even hungrier. So, doing as I was told, I always ate every morsel of food on my plate. I was a stellar, five-star member of the clean plate club. Unfortunately, because I never wasted food, my waist got bigger and bigger.

At one point, my Jennie Craig consultant suggested that if I was feeling the need to feed starving children, and this was causing me to overeat, every time I left some food on my plate in a restaurant I could donate a canned good or two to the local food pantry. This served two purposes: the first was I did not have this insane need to clean my plate and second, by leaving some food on my plate I knew I would go home and put aside a food item for the local pantry. With my new Trophy Wife Diet, I am committed to leaving at least four forkfuls of food on my plate at the end of every restaurant meal.

Tracking my calorie intake and maintaining between 1200 and 1500 calories per day was key. This along with increasing my water intake to at least six cups a day helped to keep me full and also was just great for my body.

Exercising three days per week became part of my regular routine. This included walking on the treadmill at four mph for one hour and doing eight-minute abs and eight-minute arms, which are videos that I've been doing for about fifteen years in my home.

I know all of these items are things that have been said over and over again, but this was actually the first time in my life that I have made a lifestyle change and plan on continuing with these healthful choices indefinitely. Who would have thought that I would start taking better care of myself than ever before? Once again, I trump cancer.

My very wise brother, Dave, has the secret to being rich and thin. His words of wisdom are, if you want to be rich, spend less than you make, and if you want to be thin, eat less than you need. Profound, isn't it.

Something occurred to me as I was struggling to regroup and

reemerge as myself. If I had *normal* (not HER2+) breast cancer, once you complete radiation you are *done*. But, you really aren't. Because I am HER2+, I would be getting chemo every three weeks until March, 2014. So the fact that my hair hadn't grown back in, I was still fat, and I was still missing my toenails seemed like just par for the course for someone going through cancer treatments. The people who are *done* when they drive home after the final (usually thirtieth) radiation treatment must feel like they are in a small boat being sent out to sea. Sadly, they are still in shambles from the treatments; fat, burnt, and bald. They are no longer cancer patients, they are survivors but may still look and feel like crap. It just doesn't seem fair. Ending cancer treatments on the day that you finish radiation must be like being kicked out of a moving car and landing three stories down over a cliff. It is not surprising that there is a high degree of depression following the end of cancer treatments.

Dr. Shin told me that they were starting to look more seriously at the help that people needed when treatments ended, understanding that it was a common problem. I felt I was justified in still babying myself, complaining occasionally, and continuing to wear my wig. After all, I was still in treatment.

One thing I found surprising was that with everything that I went through, surgeries, chemos, radiation, etc. I never spent a night in the hospital. My perception of a person having cancer was that you would spend many nights in the hospital, but not in my case. If I had a mastectomy, or my cancer was found later, it might have been a different story.

As it turned out, my thirtieth high school class reunion was scheduled for September. Although I was not very popular in high school, I always chose to attend reunions and usually had a great time. A private Facebook page was set up for planning and informational purposes. When I decided that I would attend the reunion with my cousin, Karen, I felt the need to make the following post so that I would not have to repeat details my current situation over and over again.

Linda Brossi Murphy posted:

"Disclaimer: I am not holding up very well. My goal for a reunion is always to be my thinnest (Even if it is only for the weekend) with beautiful hair, and minimized wrinkles—Not quite the case—Fair warning, I am bald, no eyelashes, no eyebrows, half my toenails are missing, I have gained twenty pounds, and my volleyball skills are lacking since I have neuropathy in my hands and feet. I have been battling breast cancer since October 2012, and I am scheduled with chemo until March 2014. UGH! I am only posting this since I hope to see all of you at the reunion,

I don't want to scare you with my grotesque appearance, and I believe this is a closed group, as I have not been publicizing this on Facebook. I am hanging in there and can't wait to see everyone for the great party!"

The reunion was held on the Cape in a compound owned by the former class president. Who knew when you were elected president of your senior class in high school that you would be saddled with planning every reunion for the rest of your life. It was a wonderful time; all of my former classmates were caring and so supportive. Through social media, we are closer than ever as a group, and I feel like I had an additional support network.

So the two people I knew fairly well who went through chemo and radiation handled this time differently. Jill, from the nail salon met me for lunch in October six days prior to the end of her radiation. She walked in and had on a baseball cap covering her short gray frizzy hair. She said she wore a wig to work but just didn't care anymore. B/C (before cancer) she said that she was totally groomed every day. Nails done (obviously), hair, makeup etc. As a similar type of person, I found it hard to believe that she could go from that to meeting me for lunch looking like her bald brother—her words, not mine.

My other friend, Susan A, whom I didn't know until years after her cancer, spoke of a "wig intervention" by her husband

and her friend to de-wig her. This, to me, sounds like torture. To rip off the hair of a bruised and battered cancer patient prematurely (before they are ready) sounds like cruel and unusual punishment. Apparently, she attended her son's bar mitzvah with the poodle look. She was too far past the wig to resort back to it, but not far enough along in the hair growth department to look and feel back to her old self.

As I prepared myself mentally to de-wig, the situation made me shudder. So when I went bald, I threw on my different wigs depending on my mood, and went about my day. Now, with the thought of giving up the security of my wig, I was panic-stricken.

First, I have never had short hair intentionally. The couple of times that I went a little extreme at the hairdressers I always regretted it and usually changed hairdressers after the incident. Why would they ever listen to me and cut off all my hair? Two times, after my wedding and after the birth of my daughter, I encouraged the hairdresser to give me a dramatic new look and then spent a couple days with my head under the covers, crying about how stupid I was to have them cut off my hair.

By now you all realize I am a little vain about how I look, so it should be no surprise how traumatic this was. Over the past couple of months, I'd had a few instances to go wigless in public. They had all been exercise classes. My friend Susan M and I tried a yoga class, and I felt the need to do the class without the wig. I'm not sure how I would have kept it on during downward facing dog, so it was for the best.

Since this was my first yoga class ever, aside from watching a Denise Austin yoga video in my basement, I was not very well versed in the practice. I did the best I could, but halfway through the class, I realized there was a little more to this than anticipated. As I was hanging upside down in one pose or another, I had the opportunity to see behind me towards the back of the class where there was a mirrored wall. To my horror, I quickly learned why they are called yoga pants and not yoga shorts. My private girly areas were blatantly exposed to all the people behind me as the loose legs of my shorts hung down. As discreetly as possible, I tried to angle my mat so that during the rest of the class the poor ladies behind me wouldn't be quite as horrified.

At the end of the class, I immediately rewigged with the hair I brought in my gym bag before leaving the room. Sue and her husband assured me that my hair was cute. A phrase which apparently fit, as it was the regular comment I received on the rare instances when I displayed my pathetic gray afro.

Dad's girlfriend, Marilyn, told me about the Livestrong program for cancer patients and survivors coming up at the YMCA in Framingham. The timing for this program corresponded perfectly with my goal and determination to get back to my old self. I didn't realize how fit I was until I wasn't fit at all anymore.

I met with a person from the Y and did a questionnaire about my treatments and current situation. I returned on my way back from radiation one afternoon, after the YMCA received Dr. Younger's consent for my participation, and I did a fitness test to determine my starting point. The test consisted of maximum weights I could press, some flexibility evaluations, and how far I could walk in six minutes. I was encouraged by the tester, as he was impressed by my starting point, and I left feeling a bit less lame than when I arrived.

The class that we took ran Monday and Wednesday afternoons for twelve weeks and came with a family membership for those three months. I found this very exciting, as I had never belonged to a gym and was curious as to what it was all about. The first class was just to get to know each other. Our class had five participants; Marilyn, Gayle, Kay, Eliette, and me. Being such a small class with a wonderful instructor, named Laura, was really perfect. It was interesting to get to know the people who would be together and the journey they had each been on, but I must admit I was not good about any type of group that spends a lot of time talking about cancer. I already had cancer;

it really sucked. I didn't like to spend a lot of time hearing about all of the other variations of torture that this disease could lead to. It was just too sad.

At the first exercise class, I took off my wig and jumped right into the program. Honestly, I was not sure if the gym was for me, but the opportunity to gain such a vast amount of knowledge and have the advantage of personal training was wonderful. Every machine was explained thoroughly, and we were given our settings so we could get the proper form with regard to our height. Little things, like on a certain weight machine to keep your wrists straight, or that the outer grips are harder than the ones closer to your body, really helped all of the class get the most out of their workout.

After the first class, one of the ladies couldn't wait to tell me how cute my hair was. Marilyn went on and on about how cute it was in my little poodle style. I guess poodles are cute. Quite frankly, the thought of looking like this made me cry. I found it harder to take off my wig than to put it on.

My mother and I did not have a good relationship. And, my mother wore her hair short and curly for many years. I happened to look very much like my mother. So now, I was not only going through cancer treatments, I also looked like my mother. I know all of you are judging me because of my poor relationship with my mother. Unfortunately it happens sometimes, and it didn't make me happy to look like someone I didn't get along with.

Knowing that at some point I needed to let go of the wig and move on, I made an appointment at 10 Newbury Street in Boston for November 12, the day I had a chemo appointment. I made it mid-September for mid-November because I figured that, with another inch of growth (half an inch per month), I might be able to stomach it. I picked the Salon at 10 Newbury, because they are the experts. Since they sell the wigs, they have seen many, many heads in various stages of baldness and would

Salon at 10 Newbury: foils, cut, and color!

probably know how to handle this very kinky chemo curl that makes me want to vomit.

As I sat in the chair at 10 Newbury Street salon, my friends gathered (of course I brought my entourage, I usually do better with the support of my friends) around me as they saw the pain on my face. Tears welled up in my eyes as I looked at this person I did not want to be.

The road to recovery was more difficult, in so many ways, than the road through cancer. Breaking down was easy compared to building myself back up. I spent a humongous amount of money at this beauty salon to take off my wig and feel miserable. The day that I took off my wig was by far the saddest day I have had throughout this entire ordeal.

For the record, I know I am wrong about my attitude with regard to cancer patients wearing wigs. (See honey, I can admit I am wrong.) I met Jill and subsequently another Linda who were also going through cancer treatments. Both of them have the exact same attitude about wearing a wig. They just don't care. Around their house, with their kids, or out at the grocery store, they just didn't feel the need to put hair on their head. It was hot and uncomfortable and unnecessary. Adding a bald picture of myself to this book was one of the more painful things that I have done.

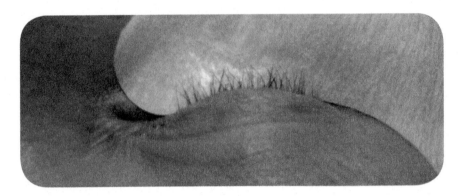

Before

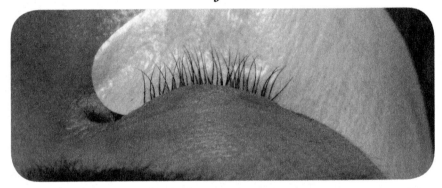

After

I learned from my new friend Jill about eyelash extensions. There was a woman named Kristie Lee at NKD salon in Worcester, who was an expert at this. In July 2013, when my lashes were just long enough, I made an appointment and had a full set of extensions put on. I told Marilyn about this beauty regime, and she came along as well and got a full set. She was so excited that for the first time in her life she has luxurious lashes. These made quite a difference in my life, and I was so excited to get rid of the time-consuming and messy false lashes that I was putting on every day. This is just one more item that helped me feel a little closer to normal.

CHAPTER 19

Tamoxifen and Neurontin

Now that radiation was complete, it was time to start on Tamoxifen. This drug has been taken for many, many years by ER/PR positive women to continue the work of the chemotherapy infusions by stripping the body of estrogen and progesterone. This medication used to be prescribed for five years, but I was told that new research indicates that staying on Tamoxifen for ten years yields better results (I assume that means helps women live longer).

Many of the women whom I've mentioned in this book, who have had cancer lite or medium, ended up being on Tamoxifen. I am the first person I have heard of who will be starting it for the ten years; most were only on for five years, and their cancer diagnoses were five years ago or longer.

Unfortunately, because I know a few women who have had experience with Tamoxifen, I was a little nervous about taking it. The complaints that I heard were depression, joint pain, foot cramps, and of course the fact that you are now in menopause, and the beauty of that is hot flashes, night sweats and decreased sex drive.

As Dr. Younger, Maria, and I were discussing that it was time for me to commence the Tamoxifen phase of my treatment, one of them suggested that I could try a drug called Neurontin, which should help with my neuropathy.

It is not advised to try two new medications at the same time, because you may have a reaction to one and then not know which one it is, we decided that I would start with Neurontin on September 10 and then ten days later start the Tamoxifen.

Neurontin and I did not get along very well. It made me very gassy (as in loud and smelly), snore like a truck driver, ditzy (I didn't have far to go from normal to ditzy anyway), gave me diarrhea, and extreme fatigue (I never slept so great in my life).

The biggest problem of all was the dulling of the nerves, which took away the pleasures of sexual intimacy.

So I gave it the old college try, but by October 3, I decided I had had enough and weaned myself off the drug. Not to bother the doctor, I went online and found out that you cannot just stop taking Neurontin, or it was dangerous, so I tapered the pills off over the course of four or five days.

In the meantime, on September 20, I began Tamoxifen. Yes, there are side effects, but not as bad as I thought they would be. For me personally, my thermostat was still out of sync. One morning, about a year after I started Tamoxifen, over the course of about an hour, I had the chills and pulled the comforter on up to the neck and snuggled in, then I was extremely hot, and I went for no covers at all, then I was a little chilly, so I put on a sheet and a blanket. I became hot again, so I went to no covers, and then I got the chills and ended up back with the comforter on. It did not end there. I repeated the cycle about three more times and then decided to get up, because there was no going back to sleep.

When I was suffering from hot flashes during Taxol treatments, I tried to explain to Dr. Younger that your whole body being engulfed in heat was extremely uncomfortable. Prior to actually having a hot flash, I must admit that I pooh-poohed the women who had these as being exceptionally dramatic. Who would think that having a rise in body temperature could be intense enough to wake you up? I will never look at a woman having a hot flash the same way again. After all, that woman could be me.

At times, I can be absolutely drenched with sweat. I can just be sitting and minding my own business and all of a sudden I get hot and sweat pours out of me. Prior to all of this I almost never sweat (even when I was stinking up the dance floor, I was not a sweater). This can be extremely embarrassing. I do realize that it is common for women who are going through menopause and have never been on Tamoxifen, to experience the same problems.

The next area of concern would be the calf and foot cramps. I've been known to leap out of bed multiple times throughout the night to walk off a foot cramp. If I look down at my foot, I can actually see how it is twisted and contorted, until I can grit my teeth and walk on it enough to loosen up the cramp.

Fortunately I have not had to deal with the issues of depression or joint pain that some of my predecessors had to deal with. Since Tamoxifen and I will be having a very long relationship, I am only glad that the side effects are not worse.

CHAPTER 20

It's October, Let's Talk Boobs

Luckily we have October. It is the month when, if you have not had enough talk about breast cancer or had enough pink in your life or enough products with pink ribbons on them, you can get your fill.

October is Breast Cancer Awareness month. During the month the American Cancer Society sponsors Making Strides for Cancer Walks around the country. These walks have been in the news every year, but that was something that other people did, and although I usually donated when asked, it was never in the forefront of my mind. Ironically, it was a year ago in the month of October that we found the lump.

As an act of support, my sister-in-law Dianne (who I should mention sent me a much appreciated card every week, for the entire year and half of my treatments) and her daughter, Amy, signed up to walk in Florida on October 20, 2013.

In Boston, Justine was busy behind the scene putting together a group to do the walk around the Charles River. Fortunately, I have started getting back into shape so when I heard that the walk was 5.7 miles along the Charles River, I said I would join in the fun. I wasn't too sure I could do it, because I was still out of shape, and the neuropathy was still a problem, but I was willing to give it the old college try.

On October 6, 2013, we took to the sidewalks of Boston with the "Love Linda" team. The team was made up of Justine and seven of her new friends from Regis College in Weston; Linda B from Boylston, and Tammy, Donna, and Kelly from my days at Assumption College in Worcester; my husband and me.

My husband dropped me off at the walk, so that I didn't have to add a longer distance to the already 5.7 miles by walking from the parking garage. Knowing a taxi was just a whistle away, I wasn't too nervous. Upon arriving, we all met near the registration area. My friend, Donna, arrived before eight, so she had time to scope out the place and purchase a great pink jacket. Who would have guessed she could get a pink thing there? When we all met up, Justine worked hard on her mission to make me cry. She made team shirts for all of the members and distributed pink beads for everyone. Then she presented me with a beautiful bracelet with my birthstones. It was amazing and so thoughtful. Smart girl knew that something pink wouldn't be the best.

During the walk there were lots of cheerleaders along the path clapping and high-fiving as we passed by. One crew of guys picked up the team names and as we approached were chanting, "Boobies, boobies," as we had been following the "Save the Boobies" team. Which as a side note, I was thinking

I couldn't care less about the boobies, but was more hopeful that we could save lives, although I do love the "Save the Ta-Tas" phrase. A bit conflicting. As we went by this group my daughter had them begin their chanting of "Linda, Linda" and I must admit it made me feel pretty good. Not sure if it was for cancer support or that a bunch of cute college guys were chanting my name. Reminded me of all those great college nights out, when the guys were all buying me drinks and begging for my attention—*ha, not*!

At the three mile potty stop, one of Justine's friends found a cell phone that was left in the porta-potty. It became my mission to return this phone to its rightful owner before leaving Boston. It was my pay-it-forward mission of the day.

We tried calling the *mom* number but couldn't hear anything, so I texted *mom,* and gave her my phone number to call back. I heard from her and through a series of follow-up calls ended up returning it to the girl near the finish line. We did a quick phone pass (without even receiving a thank you!) and continued on our way. It was my good deed for the day. I know if one of my kids lost their phone, I would really appreciate someone helping them get it back.

As we neared the end of the walk, we had the great joy of joining a group of actual cheerleaders in a robust chicken dance. It was lots of fun and really added a lot to the day. The only way it could have been better is if it was followed by the hokey-pokey.

Just after crossing the finish line, David Jr. caught up with us. He had been walking with a group from his company at Forrester Research called Fit Forr Life.

The American Cancer Society did a wonderful job with this day. It went very smoothly and was a fun way to raise awareness and money for the fight against cancer. The only thing that strikes me as a little weird, which is that we keep raising money to cure cancer, and quite frankly I would rather prevent cancer. I wish we had the magic pill that would stop the cell mutations that lead to cancer in the first place.

CHAPTER 21

This Whole Thing Is Getting Old!

December 22, 2013—Christmas was in the air. The family all gathered and decorated the tree in a Norman Rockwell fashion: drinking hot cocoa, eating popcorn, and listening to Christmas carols. The thought of my cancer never entered my mind, even though I knew that Herceptin and Pertuzumab were on the schedule for the next day.

After a dinner with all the fixings eaten in the dining room, I headed up to sort laundry and change the beds. When I was changing my daughter's bed, I scraped my hand on a notebook on the side of her bed. I found her book of poetry with the last poem written in June 2013. Being a mom and curious (aka nosey), I read it. It was a poem about me and my situation. Through teary eyes I read that a comment I made with reference to a cancer reoccurrence was quoted, "I am never going through treatments again," and how that comment really disturbed her.

How devastating it would be for her to go through graduation from nursing school, her wedding, having babies, and the rest of life's most important moments without her mother, her best friend. It really brought to the forefront that I needed to live. Not for me, but for the people who love me, whose lives would be forever scarred by my death. My father, losing a child no matter what the age; my husband, although he is a great catch and could find another woman with ease, it would be starting over without the history and memories, my children...that speaks for itself.

On Monday, two of my children, Doug and Justine, drove me to chemo. David Jr. was back to work after being home with us for the weekend. Arriving for my one o'clock appointment, I was pleased when the medical assistant, who took my vitals, told me I was down seven pounds from my last visit three weeks earlier. I think what worked was the change of diet and regular exercise, calorie counting, my Jennie Craig consultant, and a new magic pill that contained four components mentioned on Dr. Oz; cayenne pepper, green coffee been extract, raspberry ketones, and white kidney bean extract. Aside from the fact that I had never been *in the zone* so completely, the weight did seem to be coming off easier than ever before!

For some reason, my chemotherapy infusion was extremely long and a bit depressing. I usually tried to make the most of every time, but the weather outside was particularly dreary, with clouds, fog, and drizzle, which made my room seem so sullen. Then the pharmacy took over two hours to generate my chemo. Apparently there was an issue with the printer, which I never thought about, but without the ability to produce the proper labels and the instruction sheets, the battery acid, *aka* medicine, couldn't be sent up to the infusion unit.

Luckily, my steadfast and star chemo supporter, Adrianne, came in for a little while and brought a mind game that helped us pass the time.

Brave?

Is a cancer patient brave? According to dictionary.com

Brave:

1. *possessing or exhibiting courage or coura- geous endurance.*

2. *making a fine appearance.*

The word brave came up many times as I went through this hellish adventure. Quite frankly, I do not consider myself brave. If someone has a choice, such as deciding whether or not to stand on the sidewalk and watch a building burn or to run into the burning building, at the risk of their life, to save someone else—I consider the person who ran into the building to be a brave person.

When I was chatting with some friends, we were having the discussion about what the first thoughts that a person has when they see a bald, obviously cancer-treated person, out and about. One of these friends contended that her first thought when she sees a bald/scarved person is that the person is brave. I argued that her first thought is that the person has cancer, not that they are brave. This of course reverts back to my theory that every time a person sees a bald woman, not so obvious with the men, that people jump to the conclusion of cancer. She did admit, after some prodding, that I was correct, prior to idolizing their bravery in her mind, she did draw the conclusion that the person was sick and undergoing treatments. After all, cancer didn't make me bald, cancer treatments did.

So, back to the concept of brave. After the assumption that the person has cancer and is undergoing treatments, we assume they are brave to go through this. Well, as I said, I didn't feel brave. Truthfully, I did make a choice. I chose to seek medical attention when my husband found the lump and not to ignore it. But my choices weren't exactly to take a risk instead of remaining safe and unscathed. My choices were closer to choosing between the grim reaper and cancer treatments. Neither is very appealing. They both really suck, but of course dying would suck more.

Now, I must confess, I acted brave. Every time I met with a doctor or medical professional, family members or friends, I faked it. I acted happy, told them I was doing great, and bit the back of my tongue really hard if I thought I might not be able to hold it together. Which, by the way, worked. Who knew that causing myself physical pain could help me keep my act together and prevent me from exposing my emotional pain? Aside from my breakdown with Dr. Shin, I was able to keep up this façade. I tried to make my radiation team think I had nothing better to do Monday through Friday for six weeks but to drive into Boston and visit them. I put a smile on my face and cookies in hand once a week and gleefully lay down so they could zap the crap out of me.

CHAPTER 22

Blood

It must sound weird, but I loved donating blood. I had been donating every eight weeks for many years, per the guidelines. My blood type is O negative, which makes me a universal donor, and it gets them all giddy when I come in to donate. It is the one that they yell for in the emergency room when they have a big emergency, and the doctor says "start the patient on O neg." One of the many reasons I love to donate is that every time I do I can save up to three lives. That is huge! Something that takes a couple of hours every eight weeks makes a huge difference for the people I was helping. Part of the donation process is to answer a series of questions to make sure that I am eligible and have not been exposed to anything that would harm the recipient of my blood. I have always found these questions to be quite annoying, but it is just part of the process, and I would rather that the blood collectors be ultra-conservative and safe, rather than endanger someone that they were trying to help.

I say this from experience. I received nine blood products, some whole blood, and some platelets in 1998 and it saved my life! After the simple procedure of a D&C, an artery had been sliced during the procedure, and I had internal bleeding and was very close to dying. I had numerous blood transfusions and emergency surgery, then spent a week in a coma while my body tried to figure out what was going on.

The good news is, eventually, I recovered and was fine. This happened when the children were quite small, and I am very grateful I was not taken from them so early. As part of my gratitude for the lifesaving blood that others gave to me I wanted to give back in return.

I can say I have. My blood donations have totaled forty-four pints until my diagnosis with cancer. At that point, you are deferred for one year. When my year was up, I started receiving phone calls again asking me to come and donate. Seeing that my treatments well exceeded the year, I was still not eligible. Morally, I am not sure I should ever donate again. Because of the aggressive nature of the HER2+ cancer that I have, I am not sure that I can know with certainty I will not be passing along a horrible disease to a person who is already so sick that they are receiving blood transfusions.

The selfish side of blood donation is that I have been using it as my personal weight loss method. Each pint of blood weighs 1.3 pounds. That is automatic weight loss. And my theory is that my body needs to work hard in order to make new blood to replace what was taken out, and this probably burns extra calories as well. All of this might be false, but I believe it. I also think that it is good for me to have fresh blood in my body. By taking out a pint and making a fresh pint to replace it, that it will increase my overall health. (Seeing that I have cancer, this could all be a bunch of hogwash.)

As soon as I was diagnosed with cancer, I contacted the American Red Cross and asked them if there was some way I could get back my last blood donation and not have it be used. I was so fearful that the HER2+ would be in that blood and be put in another person's body. That blood was used before I was diagnosed, and it was too late. My other thought was did I get

CHAPTER 23

· ·

Grrrr, He's Driving Me Crazy!

My absolutely wonderful husband was driving me crazy, and I was not sure I wanted to be married to him anymore. I do know that out of the twenty-eight years we have been married, there have been absolutely wonderful times, and I would not throw this away quickly and lightly. I had been in treatment for over a year when David went away skiing with some friends, and while he was gone I enjoyed my time alone home so much. Unfortunately, absence was not making the heart grow fonder. So I had a couple of choices. I could research divorce attorneys or marriage counselors.

Because overall, I feel like we've had an amazing marriage, I chose the latter. I found a couple who does three-day counseling up in Vermont and inquired. For the nominal fee of $8,000, David and I could be fixed over a three-day span. A little pricy!

Interestingly, on the website it stated that during certain points in a marriage a tune up might be required. These transition points were things like losing a beloved pet, a major illness, empty nesting, having a college graduate move out on his own, and of course the good old midlife crisis. Did I mention David and I are both forty-eight? And it didn't say it, but I had been thrown into medically induced menopause, which could not be helping the situation. Having read this, I breathed a sigh of relief. Yay! We were normal. We are supposed to be struggling a little bit when we are going through every item on the marriage stressor list.

Because I did not feel our marriage was in bad enough shape to warrant the $8,000 expenditure, I went about my own brand of marriage counseling. I got a large bulletin board out of the basement and began making charts of all of our problems. I also made a list of hot button items that I never wanted to talk about again. (An example of this would be how messy my desk is. It is extremely messy and unorganized—always has been and always will be a mess—no need to ever talk about this again.) They are things that we have discussed over and over again for more than twenty-nine years.

One of the sheets of paper was an overreaction chart. Going through life there are items that require a one response, such as spilling a glass of milk, and items that require a ten response such as you have cancer. I must admit, David and I are both guilty of overreacting and ramping up about little things that shouldn't matter. A situation that barely required a comment would escalate into a ridiculous fight about nothing. Out of respect for David, I will not get into the nitty-gritty of the chart.

When David got home and saw our marriage counseling bulletin board, he received it quite well, as he also had been frustrated with our current level of harmony. Our marital disharmony was just another way that cancer sucked!

Of course, as I was making the chart, I was pretty sure I was blameless. After all, I was merely a victim of cancer who should be treated with kid gloves. So, it was a little bit of a blow to know that David had some sheets that he wanted to add to the board about my inadequacies. I took it like an adult and got some sheets out and added more to our reality-check board.

Apparently, when I imitated him with a pruned-up face and a head shake, and used a squeaky voice to make fun of him, that bothered him. Who knew?

Also, as I mentioned before, I am a bit loud. I have every conversation in my life either on the phone or in person as if the person I am speaking with is severely hard of hearing. David calls this yelling, but I tell him it is merely speaking loudly, and being Italian. Sheepishly, I realized that I was probably not only offending David with my loud volume but other people I interact with as well. I was committed to trying to lower my volume and stay off the reality-check board.

One of the sheets that I added to the board was that I no longer wanted to discuss divorce as an option in our life. I was making the choice that working on our marriage was the only choice. I truly adore my husband and want to grow old with him, which at this point is a struggle unto itself, seeing that my life could be cut short by cancer. I want to play with our grandchildren together and sit holding his hand at each of our children's weddings. So divorce is not an option in our life, and I made a sheet to ensure that we never discussed it again. Both of us had a weight lifted off of our shoulders, knowing that without renewing our vows, we had recommitted to each other in a deeper, more sincere way than ever before.

We did not make it twenty-four hours before we had to write on the board. We ended up in a fight about peanut-butter bars. This was the exact problem that we had been having, which was a ridiculous fight about a ridiculous situation. So I got out the pen and listed under our overreaction caption how we escalated a discussion about peanut-butter bars into a full-blown fight.

It did not feel good to write this down on the board and know that we were wasting our time and happiness on silly arguments. So now that the board was christened, neither of us wanted to have our inadequacies written down. This had the exact effect I was hoping for. It felt like we were getting detention back in high school when our mistakes were put down on paper. Neither of us wanted our inadequacies noted on this permanent record.

My husband and I are both very driven, hardworking, intense people. Because of this, I can think of almost no situation in life that he and I don't both have a very strong opinion. We are also competitive which keeps both of us behaving, so that the other will be written up on the board more than we are. This determination to be on our best behavior ultimately leads to a better relationship.

Over the course of our marriage, we have had two other theories that we have turned to frequently to help keep our relationship on track. They are the *spiral-up, spiral-down theory* and *the marble jar theory*. The spiral-up, spiral-down theory was created by my husband. Basically, it is based on the fact that a person's behavior often tends to follow another's. So if I do something mean to my husband, he will then do something mean to me, so then I will do something hurtful to him, and so on. On the other hand, if you find yourself in a spiral-down pattern you can reverse that by starting the spiral-up pattern. During the spiral-up pattern my husband will do something kind, considerate, and thoughtful, then I will try to trump that with something even more kind, considerate, and thoughtful, and now both of us are being so damn nice to each other some of our friends are probably ready to gag!

I know the spiral theory sounds quite rudimentary, but it is amazing how great it works, even with the kids. If one of them is doing poorly at school, or is grouchy, one of us will pick them up, bring them out to dinner and a movie, and give them some extra-special attention. The tough thing about changing from the spiral down to the spiral up is that when you're in the spiral down you usually are not feeling too great about the person, so it takes a lot of strength to reverse the spin.

The marble theory, authored by my father, relates to the fact that every relationship has a marble jar. Each person in that relationship has a jar of marbles that is their view on the relationship. Let me demonstrate by example. I had a friend whom I absolutely adored. However, over and over again this person let me down. She promised to call and never called, she did not get in touch with me, except for a couple times, over the year and half of cancer treatments. She would cancel plans last minute, etc.

At the beginning of our relationship, we were having a great time. We would head out for dinner and five hours later still be talking and laughing as the waitstaff stood by with their arms crossed, tapping their feet. The great times put marbles into my marble jar connected to this relationship/friend. Then, each time she let me down marbles were taken out of the jar. Because I adore this woman, and we had so many fun times together, there were a lot of marbles in the jar. However, because of the excessive number of times, recently, that she was not a true friend, her jar was down to almost no marbles. I have made the choice not to do any more work towards our relationship, unless she puts some more marbles in through consideration and caring acts.

So, when my husband and I are spiraling up, if we are exceptionally nice to each other, we will refer to the fact that the other person just put more marbles in the jar.

In my father's theory, once your marble jar is 100 percent depleted, the relationship is over. I happen to agree with this, because you can only forgive so much, and if no one is adding any good to your life, or marbles to your jar, it is time to move on.

The board is still up, and luckily we do not need to write on it very often, because merely being aware of our own behaviors has helped us fine tune our interactions.

CHAPTER 24

A Hiccup on the Road to Rebuilding Myself

A big speed bump in my road to recovery occurred February 7. I had been moving right along prior to this day. It was with great pride that I started the week by doing twenty plank push-ups on Monday. This was the first time that I was able to do these since my body fell into disrepair. Starting the Tuesday after Labor Day, I was only able to do push-ups on my knees and with great effort. My goal was to get back to twenty plank push-ups as part of my Monday, Wednesday, Friday exercise schedule.

On Facebook, I saw a post about people trying a plank challenge. Knowing how great planks are for my core, back, and arms, I decided to jump on board and start the challenge. So in December, I printed out the plank challenge calendar and attempted to do this, hopefully with my husband by my side. I thought it would be great for both of us and our future health. This failed miserably. I was waiting every day for us to do this together. One thing led to the next, and we missed more days than we planked. So, I decided to try it again the middle of January when life slowed down a little bit after the holidays.

I once again printed out the thirty-day plank challenge. This time I was more committed, and printed it on bright yellow paper to grab my attention. Well, success. I was becoming the plank queen. It started out with twenty seconds for a few days and then increased from there with a couple days of rest here and there.

So there I was rolling along. Monday I did twenty plank push-ups along with two minutes of planking. Wednesday I did my twenty push-ups and two minutes and thirty seconds of planking and Thursday I planked for two and a half minutes as well. Just to be clear, this is very hard to do. My whole body was quivering by the end of this time frame, and I know it really is a challenge to be able to plank for five minutes at the end of thirty days. Even though it was difficult, I was committed.

Friday morning my husband David, my son, Doug, his friend, Teddie, and I all decided to head for the slopes at Sunday River in Maine. I had been skiing two times over the past few months and bought a new pair of skis. This new pair replaced my twenty-year-old parabolic skis which had replaced the then-twenty-year-old set I had from childhood, which actually had a strap you tied around your ankle to keep your ski from skiing away without you if you fell. Needless to say, I was very excited to unleash my inner athlete and strut my stuff on the slopes. After all, I was feeling much better, I had lost a lot of weight, my hair was almost looking like a style, and I was getting in great shape.

We arrived at the slopes, and I was on fire. These new skis had lulled me into believing that I actually had some talent, and I was doing my best to keep up with the rest of my group. It was a bit chilly (it is skiing, after all) and Teddie, and I headed in for a cup of coffee. After a short break, we rejoined my husband and son, and we headed back up the chairlift to an intermediate slope. I was feeling really great about my new skis, as I had never done so well on any ski before. As I got into my groove and my mojo was on fire, I vigorously made a turn to the left, pole outstretched, with body fully engaged. At that moment, my right boot popped out of my ski, and I flew through the air as if I was untethered from the earth. I felt myself falling. Next thing I knew, I was lying on the snowy slopes.

I always wondered if you would know if you really hurt yourself, or if you could hurt yourself and not realize it until later. Well, I had my answer: if you really hurt yourself, you would know it. Doug's friend was behind me, and she came upon my yard sale (the affectionate term used when a person unintentionally sheds all of their ski equipment and spreads it out all over the mountain). After realizing that I wasn't going to pop right back up and put my skis on to get down the mountain, she called for ski patrol, and let the guys know I was down for the count.

As I was lying on the mountain, I realized that I was in some of the worst pain of my life. I couldn't decide if I had broken my arm or dislocated my shoulder, but I knew for sure I had done something very, very bad to myself. I have no memory of actually hitting the ground. I only remember falling and then lying on the mountain in extreme pain.

My very helpful ski patrolman, Pete, put a sling on my arm and helped roll me into the sled of shame. For some reason, Teddie thought it was a great idea to preserve the moment and took a picture as I was pulled downhill towards morphine.

I vaguely heard Pete tell my husband the game plan as we passed by him while I was paralyzed by pain, each bump in the sled shooting through me like swords. Until this event, I thought I had a high pain tolerance. Right about then I was doubting that self-evaluation. At the ski patrol office, the goal was to extricate me from my clothes. That would be all five layers. As I mentioned it was very cold out. Some things came off easily, and others were just not worth the effort. When we got down to the Under Armor and thermal underwear, I told them to cut them off. Saving the shirts were not worth the pain. While all this was going on, I think I asked for morphine at least a dozen times. This was some of the worst pain of my life. When my husband joined the party, before he knew how bad it was, he asked if I wanted him to bring me home so we could go to our local ER. When he noticed the tearstained cheeks, he realized that wasn't a viable option.

When the ski patrol was done stripping me, they sent me over to the clinic, which was a medical facility twenty feet away equipped with an RN, a PA, and an X-ray machine and tech. It did not take a brain surgeon to know I dislocated my shoulder; even my husband figured it out by looking at the bulge of shoulder protruding from my back. Luckily still under the skin.

I was a little disappointed that they didn't have what was needed to access my port. That would have been a nice bonus for the cancer patient with the hurt shoulder. The saint of an RN worked for a while and eventually found a vein to give me some morphine. As he worked diligently to find the vein, I was grateful that I'd had the port in place and didn't need to go through this hunt and peck procedure during each and every chemo. It wouldn't surprise me if everyone there thought I was a junkie; I was begging for morphine. The one other time in my life that I was in dire pain, morphine did the trick.

I think that this RN was being a little stingy; although I was getting some morphine, I wasn't as pain-free as I wished. However, I was pain-free enough to go into the X-ray room for my photo shoot. The tech took a couple of pictures. As she was developing them, they had me lie down on a gurney with my dislocated left arm hanging off the bed. Jerry, the physician's assistant, approached my bad arm, and I could tell from the look in his eye I was in for a treat. Time to put the shoulder back into its socket. Time was of the essence. It is my understanding that if your shoulder stays out of the socket for more than an hour, the ligaments and tendons could be permanently damaged. We were slightly past the one-hour mark since my fall. As Jerry gently began to manipulate my arm back into place, the X-ray tech asked him to take a look at my films before he began. His words, "Please give her some more morphine" made it clear to me that this was getting serious!

It turned out that I don't do anything halfway. Not only did I have a dislocated shoulder, I also fractured the top knob of my humerus. Let me assure you, this was not humorous at all! Well, Jerry was a pro. The pain was excruciating, even after a boatload of morphine. David knew that it really hurt when he saw tears pouring down my face as the PA torqued the broken bone into its proper position. The post "push a broken bone back into its socket" pictures showed how nicely the broken bone went back into place. Instructions were to follow up with an orthopedic surgeon, because I might need surgery. UGH!

When you are a cancer patient your mind tends to default to the possibility that any problem you are having could be cancer related. David and I discussed later that each of us had the thought that my bone broke because my cancer had metastasized and this was an indication of a bigger problem. Luckily that was not the case.

This whole experience unto itself was a real big pain. Luckily, it was my left arm. David said that if it were my right arm, he would have dropped me off at rehab on the way home, because he knew how useless I would be. The kicker in this whole ordeal was the cancer. My broken shoulder was like adding a tornado to an already dark and stormy night.

It turned out after a trip to the shoulder specialist—yes, there is actually a shoulder department at Mass General—I did not need surgery. I was so relieved that this situation had not gone from bad to worse. I think we need to change the name of the hospital from Massachusetts General Hospital to Massachusetts Specialized Hospital. There is a specialist for almost any specific body part or disease. The reasons I made the trip into Boston for my shoulder were twofold. First, I wanted to keep my care all in one place, so if I needed surgery, it could be coordinated all under one roof. The second reason was, when I was researching shoulder doctors and I saw that Mass General actually has a person who only works on shoulders, I figure that I wouldn't be his first rodeo if I needed surgery, and he probably knew what he was doing.

Guess what you do with two hands. Yep, everything. If I

needed to do this stupid thing, at least I hurt my left shoulder and not my right, or things would have been much worse.

This brings me to an interesting observation. I have gone through my life corralling the boobies by putting my bra on my arms and reaching in back and hooking my bra. Hence, the current problem of getting my bra snapped any day that David was up and out of the house before I was dressed as he would have the job of clasping my bra for me.

A physical therapist friend of mine, also a cancer survivor, looked at me like I had two heads and asked me why I didn't just snap my bra in the front and twist it around and then put my arms through? Brilliant! This thought never occurred to me. Then as I was expounding to anyone who would listen about this new way one could put on their bra, the consensus was that at least half (maybe more) of my friends were already putting on their bras in this manner.

So this leads me to the big question. Were we actually taught this in our budding prepubescent state by our mothers? Is it a flexibility issue? Why don't women who snap their bras in the front just buy front clasping bras? This whole snapping in the front, and twirling it around was awkward and time-consuming, but at least I didn't need to get help from the UPS man (even though we all know how sexy they are in their brown uniforms).

CHAPTER 25

Nearing the End of Treatments

On February 25 I headed to Boston with my friend
Linda B for my second-to-last chemo. It is bittersweet. I truly wanted to be all better and move on
from this horrible disease. However, I have made
having cancer such a party, between the joy on
people's faces when I gave them cookies to having
such quality time with so many of my wonderful
family and friends.

I have grown extremely fond of the nurses and the staff at MGH, and quite frankly, I was going to miss them when this was all over.

We started out the afternoon with lunch at the Clink restaurant in the Liberty Hotel. It was a restaurant my friend Linda had never been to but was on her list. We had a great meal and some yummy wine. When we were headed back into the

On Facebook:
Linda B wrote: "Who says there isn't any
help out there for assholes?"

hospital, we came across the following poster and had to post it on Facebook. The tagline that Linda came up with to go along with this poster had me laughing for days.

On this day I had a new nurse for chemo. Her name was Anne, and she was very nice. Being a creature of habit who does not like change, I was a little upset that instead of my regular nurse and my regular area of treatment, I would be thrust into a new environment so close to the end. I requested that George be my nurse, since I was familiar with him, and it would put me in my regular unit. However there was some glitch in the system, and they had written that I requested not to have George in the future.

I'm not sure why this information was written down, as it had nothing to do with how I felt, and quite honestly anytime Lorraine was not around I wanted to have George, to whom I had grown quite attached. The last time I had been to MGH, they had scheduled my last three appointments with George, and I had said I did not want George, I wanted Lorraine.

Apparently this information was misconstrued, and they made a note to that effect. Hopefully, my last treatment could be with George, since Lorraine would not be able to treat me. The good news was that she should be back in an administrative capacity, so I would be able to see her.

The reason I had Anne was because Lorraine fell on the ice while walking her dog. She broke her right wrist and had to have surgery the Friday before my appointment. Unfortunately, that meant that she would not be my nurse at my last chemo appointment either. I couldn't believe that I'd been down such a long road with her by my side and would not have her with me as I finished this journey. Since the day we met her, and she discussed the benefits of saran wrap, straight through my thirty-seven-pound weight gain and numerous side effects, she had been a mainstay for me, making me laugh while caring for me and delivering my battery acid with a smile on her face.

During chemo, I texted Lorraine, and when I found out she was available to talk, I gave her a call right away. This is the kind of relationship she and I have, where I even had her personal cell phone number. If we lived closer to each other, I think we would become good friends outside of MGH.

Later in the day, Michelle, my college roommate, and Justine came in to join the party. Because Michelle had business in Boston the following day, she booked a hotel for us to stay in. So after chemo, the four of us went out to dinner at a pub across the street from the hospital. Of course this dinner involved some more wine, and I enjoyed the wonderful company of these three very important women in my life. Although the main activity and reason for going to Boston was quite scary, because we have had so much fun on the road through this horrible disease, I'd been filled with far more laughs and smiles than tears and pain.

On February 27, I headed into Boston again, as I continued on my road to recovery. Today I was scheduled to have the first laser treatment to remove my radiation tattoos with Dr. Tsao, and a follow-up appointment with Dr. Warner regarding my broken shoulder. I arrived for my 2:30 laser treatment. I went into the waiting room and sat down, and the woman to my left was 100 percent bald. Honestly, it made me totally uncomfortable,

My heart was saddened for this person, and because I absolutely knew what she's going through, my heart was bleeding for her; I know the pain of the journey. Seeing somebody without a wig was painful. I thought selfishly that if she had had the wig on, I would not have known what she was going through, and I would have been more comfortable.

Thinking back to that discussion about believing people were strong when you see them going through cancer— that was not my reaction. My reaction was empathy and pain on her behalf. Because this was a dermatology office, not a cancer clinic, it was out of context and had an entirely different impact on me. I regularly saw bald people on the eighth and ninth floors at Yawkey and lots of cue balls in the radiation waiting room, but no one quite as bald out of the confines of the place where you know everyone has cancer.

David and I were out and about one day and met a new neighbor. During the conversation, he mentioned my very obviously injured arm. I told him that I felt like the Book of Job from the Bible, with so many things going wrong in my life recently.

I proceeded to tell him it all started September 26, 2012. My four-legged companion, Toby, had to be put to sleep because of cancer. On October 2, 2012, we found the lump. I pulled my back out on October 22, 2012. I was diagnosed with cancer November 7. I subsequently had two surgeries (the second one for clean margins), chemo, radiation, a crazy replacement dog we had to return to its breeder, my mother-in-law diagnosed with congestive heart failure, and now a dislocated and broken shoulder.

Surprisingly he didn't just run away from us fearing that my bad luck might rub off on him. He looked at me thoughtfully and mused that my life could actually be the inspiration for the lyrics of a great country song.

On March 18, I woke early for my last day of chemo. My emotions ran between exhilaration and trepidation. After nearly a year and a half from the fateful lump-finding, it was now time to close this chapter. David and I started out the morning in an argument. We quarreled on many of the mornings when David was my driver to chemo.

It wasn't until we reflected upon how things had evolved, when we were creating our marriage board, that we realized the cause of so many arguments was the stress of him bringing me to chemo. I think I can understand that. What man wants to watch someone he loves go through so much? It has to be extremely nerve-racking. And I know that he wants me to live, so this entire cancer situation hurt him on so many levels.

Really? I couldn't believe that this was the final day to get infused with battery acid. I was a little sad that Lorraine wouldn't be my nurse. I felt like we started this together and I really would have loved to finish it with my lively, lovely friend. Her broken wrist relegated her to triage duty.

Apparently I was supposed to start the day at 8:00 a.m. with labs. Oops, I missed that part and thought it was to start at 8:45 with Dr. Younger. Needless to say, I arrived later than 8:45 then was sent for labs and didn't see the doctor until 9:45. One hundred percent my fault. I wanted to blame Lauren, my research coordinator, but Justine backed her and remembered that I was supposed to arrive at eight. Oh well, I knew they couldn't start without me. How bad is it that I was more punctual for my hair appointments than my chemo? It's all about priorities.

So I checked in for labs and dropped off what I hoped was my last cookie plate ever to reception. Although the folks in the front check-in area aren't the key to my care, it had been nice to make their day by dropping off cookies. The cookies have replaced my blue card at Mass General. By bringing cookies every time I just had to smile and hand over a plate of cookies and the person at the desk immediately said, "Hi, Linda!" It has been the ultimate health care passport.

I was excited to report that I weighed in at 132 pounds. Yeah! This was less than the 136 pounds that I weighed on November 15, 2012, which was my first Mass General appointment after I was pumped full of those ridiculous testosterone pills. So I had come full circle with my weight—up thirty-plus pounds, down thirty-plus pounds. As you can see in the pictures in this book, I fully blew up like a balloon then luckily deflated.

So all was good with my labs. I had a delightful nurse access my port before George arrived for the day. I gave up five tubes of blood (no wonder cancer patients are anemic) and some urine to seal the deal. While we were chatting, I mentioned the cookies. She asked if I was Lorraine's patient, because she had heard of me (once again, the power of cookies is amazing). I then explained to her how Lorraine and I bonded over saran wrap. When she finished laughing, she gave me a contemplative look and told me there actually is a thing made for safe oral sex called a dental dam. You learn something new every day.

While waiting for my appointment, my friend Heidi W arrived with a big bouquet of pink balloons. I felt like announcing, "it's a girl!' Just kidding. They were so festive they really were a great reminder that this was a joyous day.

This really helped because prior to Heidi's arrival Justine came in, and we looked at each other and started to cry. Not sure why, but seeing my daughter brought all of the emotions of the day to the surface.

For levity we observed the art work that adorned the walls of the waiting room and changed each month. Follow me on this tangent. The father of my friend Anne from Texas was dying of lung cancer. He was in her house and not doing very well. Anne went in to check on him, and his skin was all orange and brown. This bizarre coloring prompted Anne to call the ambulance. She was thinking that he might have fallen. His face was all black and blue, or perhaps he had some rare reaction to a medication, or maybe his blood was too thin and was causing bruising. Very scary. After several hours in the ER and multiple tests, someone wiped her dad's face, and the brown substance came off. Anne knew this must be one of the many hijinks her mother could have pulled. After pushing for an answer, she found out it was turmeric, which her mother had rubbed all over her father because it apparently cures cancer. Once again, who knew?

Unfortunately this was not a miracle cure, and Anne's dad passed away in March 2012. This story did lighten my spirits in the waiting room, as there was a picture of turmeric, which looked quite phallic and caused me to crack up, since I have the maturity level of a ten-year-old boy.

When we were called into the exam room, we didn't have to wait long to see Dr. Younger. He entered and his face lit up. I'm not sure if it was me or the amazing plate of cookies Heidi M had made for him. (I know it really was the cookies.)

This was my last appointment as a cancer patient. Yeah! Which of course led to the question of what I was now. Was I cured? In remission? A survivor? I needed to know. Dr Younger said I was in 100 percent remission. (Not sure there is such thing as 100 percent remission, but I liked the sound of it.) He was not a fan of the word survivor, and he said cured wasn't the right word either.

On the television show *Parenthood*, when Christina was done with her treatments, she had a scan and got to get an A+ in health. Unfortunately, this wasn't the case in the real world. Dr. Younger said that the scan isn't that accurate, and he felt the exposure to the radiation wasn't worth it. I told him I would let him get away with that answer for now, but I might change my mind by the next visit and insist on it.

I was excited to learn that he was going to be coming to the thank-you party I was planning. I felt so honored that my oncologist, with his busy schedule, would drive out to central Massachusetts for the party. Of all the amazing people I want to thank, he is near, or perhaps at, the top of the list. Although his orders and protocols put me through the ringer, hopefully they have saved my life. Who needs toenails anyway?

After the pow-wow with David, Justine, Dr. Younger, and me, we headed downstairs for my final Yawkey 8E event. I had grown so close to so many people on my team, it was bittersweet to be leaving them with the ultimate hope never to return.

George was my nurse, and I was so happy, because after the misunderstanding a few weeks ago, I wanted to be sure he understood how fond I am of him. Poor George could barely do his job, because my room was so crowded. For my final chemo, I was blessed to have a full entourage. The final chemo act con-sisted of my husband, David, son, Doug, daughter, Justine, and friends Adrianne, Michelle, Heidi W, Tammy M, and Kelly. I knew most people were coming, but Kelly and Tammy were an added surprise.

I was so anxious, it seemed to take forever for my chemo to arrive. Of course this would not have been the case had I showed up for labs at eight as I was supposed to. The schedule was for me to have my port removed at two o'clock. As the time was ticking, it was obvious that I was not going to be able to make this appointment and I called to push it up. Luckily this wasn't a problem. I was grateful, because I really wanted to wrap up this saga today.

A bag of Herceptin, followed by a bag of Pertuzumab or placebo, and chemo would be done. The time passed quickly, surrounded by family and friends. I was so grateful for such an amazing support system. During treatment, Lauren and Maria visited me. Maria entertained us with adorable videos of her son, Hunter, (who was now over a year old) and Lauren gave me an amazing card. It cracked me up, because she stated that she hoped she never saw anyone paint their toe skin like toenails again. I didn't know if Lauren had such a close bond with all of her patients, but I felt very special.

Big mistake of the day was not wearing the sling on my arm, which was healing, although still quite painful, and had been out of the sling for about a week. Clearly when people are happy for you, they give you big enthusiastic hugs. Because I kept

Maria and Linda

George and Linda

raising my right arm, they raised their right arms and squeezed my broken shoulder with vim and vigor. Ouch! By the time I exited the infusion ward, my shoulder was in excruciating pain, and I was walking around like my left broken shoulder was attached to my ear.

We parted company from half of the entourage in the lobby, so they could head home, while I went to be de-ported. I found the schedule at Mass General to work out well for the most part (aside from the shoulder clinic, which could run hours behind schedule); we didn't have to wait too long for any of my procedures. Michelle, Doug, and Justine settled in while I prepared to close this chapter. My husband had chipped a tooth and needed to leave earlier to have it repaired at the dentist. Michelle was going to drive me back home, so that my kids could go back to college.

The infusion port removal procedure went as smoothly as possible. As it turned out, the nurse who prepped me for the procedure had three daughters at Regis College, also studying nursing, and Justine knew the one who was also a freshman. Talk about a small world.

Once again, the procedure was performed with the patient wide awake, and this time I knew there was no happy juice involved. There was local pain medication that quite frankly did not do the trick. This had already been a very long day, and I couldn't wait for the procedure to be over and this nightmare to be done.

When I was back in my clothes we headed out for dinner and then homeward bound. Hallelujah!

Prior to cancer I never took pain medicine. I took a birth control pill, and asthma and allergy medicines but followed my grammy's lead. If I had a headache, I would drink some water and lie down. Of course this is quite easy for me, because I have been blessed with a very high pain tolerance and very little pain in my life. Since cancer, my philosophy has changed. This is because I have had a lot of pain between surgeries and my broken shoulder. Since I have been regularly pumped so full of toxic chemicals, I figured, what difference is a little codeine going to make in my system?

That night when I got home from my last day of chemo I felt like a total invalid. My left arm was still useless and I had an incision on the right side of my chest, with strict instructions not to do any heavy lifting or exercise for seven days. I had decided to do all of the food prep for the thank you party myself. I now pictured myself gripping a butcher knife between my teeth and bobbing my head up and down over the cutting board to chop the chicken for the casserole I was making.

Lying in bed that night I felt trapped. My left shoulder was still broken and sore, so I couldn't lie on my left side. My right side had an incision from the port removal that afternoon so I couldn't lie on my right side, and I can never sleep on my stomach or I get a backache (that doesn't make sense to me, but that is what happens.). So I was on my back and in pain. I was totally imprisoned staring at the ceiling. Even the codeine that I had taken couldn't lull me back to sleep, because I was entombed by pain and injury and couldn't move.

I have mentioned a thank-you party a couple of times. This

was the brainchild of Michelle. First of all she knows how much I like a good party. I've done my best to make cancer as fun as possible for myself and others. As I was lamenting about all of the thank-you notes I needed to write for the countless gifts, books, games, cards, rides in and out of Boston, company through so many chemo and radiation treatments, meals, edible arrangements, donations to the Love Linda team, and so many other thoughtful gestures, Michele suggested that I thank everybody in person.

One of my favorite gifts was the blanket with the picture of my family on it, which I was wrapped in after each surgery and during every infusion. I also wore the prayer shawl around my shoulders, which was presented to me by Sandy from her church. My friend Susan E, who spent a few afternoons with me on Yawkey 8E gave me a cheerleading teddy bear with "Go, Linda!" on the front. I called it my "chair/cheerful/cheerleading bear." Marilyn made me a wonderful bathrobe

which was so comfortable and snuggly during my chemo comas and beyond.

One final gift was given to me further along in the process by my friend Karyn, who sadly lost both of her parents over the last couple of years to cancer. She gave me a CD with a series of songs on it that related to our friendship and also a few of those feel-good "I am woman" kinds of songs such as *I Will Survive,* (Hope Karyn is right about this) Alicia Keys' *Girl on Fire*, and Brandi Carlile's *The Story* along with songs by U2, to remind me of our very fun trip to Miami and *How Great Thou Art* by Ronan Tynan which can move me to tears.

David's cousin, Cathy, sent me three themed packages, which were fun and unique. One was for St. Patrick's Day, another had a winter theme, and then there was a fun-in-the-sun package packed in a little cooler.

There are too many gifts and thoughtful acts to name in this short book. But hopefully the thank-you party was a way of letting people know how much I appreciate everything that they did.

The party was scheduled for March 23, an open house the Sunday after my last treatment. There were many people that I wanted to thank personally for doing so much over the course of the year and a half.

On Saturday, Nancy, Linda B, and Heidi M came over to help me prepare the food, since I was crippled on my right side from the incision and my left side because of the broken shoulder. They did a wonderful job, and by the time they left my house on Saturday, everything for the party was cooked and set up.

The party was lots of fun and a great success! Heidi M got a chance to say hello to Dr. Younger, who had also been her oncologist.

People ate, drank, and socialized during the afternoon, and it was wonderful to be able to show my appreciation the way I liked to best.

My father, David, Marilyn, and Dr. Jerry Younger

Although this officially, I hope, ends my cancer saga, my life will be forever altered by this experience.

Linda, all better, with Dr. Younger!

EPILOGUE

It is amazing, it has only been six months since my final cancer treatment and it is already a distant memory. When you're in the bowels of such an all-encompassing, dramatic life crisis, it is incomprehensible that you will ever be "normal" again. My hair is a normal style. My tattoos are much lighter and after a couple more treatments they will be gone. I weigh less now than I did before David found the lump. I am back to exercising and working like the whole year and a half nightmare never existed.

The toenails are still being a bother and will require some attention, as they are becoming ingrown, as they slowly (and I mean slowly) start to grow out and my left boobie is still about one and a half times the size of my right.

The end of March, about a week after I finished treatments, my mother-in-law and one of my best friends, Betty Murphy, took a turn for the worse and entered hospice. For the final week of her life until she passed on April 5, David and I were by her side. During one of her more lucid moments, I shared with her that I had finished all of my treatments and I was 100 percent all better. It gave me such joy and happiness to let her know that for now, I was going to be okay. We embraced and held each other for a long time. I am so lucky that I was able to share the news that I finished my treatments with her before she passed away. My diagnosis of cancer was devastating to her, and I know my treatments were a very difficult time for her, as she worried and prayed daily. Regret lingers that we never got to go on that cruise the year before. F*ck off, cancer! You robbed me of that wonderful experience I would've had with one of my favorite people in the whole world.

Now that the dust has settled, David and I are going to enjoy empty nesting more fully this year, without the distraction of regular trips to MGH. We still have our reality-check marriage board available, if needed, but with all of the extra stressors taken out of our day-to-day life, we are so much happier.

Dr. Younger and Dr. Smith are keeping me on a leash, with follow-up visits, 3-D MRIs, and echocardiograms to be sure I am as healthy as I feel.

Cancer sucks! But if it does not kill you, and you get better, it has a beginning, a middle, and an end, and then you can go on living. For me, it was just a lump in the road. Let's hope I am right!

Before: At a family wedding, August 2012

During...Fuck Off, Cancer!

After

About the Author

Linda Brossi Murphy is a married, mother of three who resides with her family just outside of Worcester, Massachusetts. She graduated from Marian High school (1983) in Framingham and has her BA from Assumption College (1987) in Worcester. She currently works for her family real estate management company and this is her first book.

Contact Linda if you would like her to skype or call into your book club discussion. fckoffcancer@gmail.com

Did you enjoy the book?

Please review it on Amazon or Good Reads with a 5 star rating.

If you didn't enjoy the book please follow Grammy Brossi's advice; "If you can't say something nice, don't say anything at all."

The thank you's associated with the writing and publication of this book are so numerous I cannot even begin to list all of the wonderful people who helped me with this endeavor. You know who you are. My endless gratitude and appreciation to all of you.

F*ck Off Cancer Book Club Discussion Questions

1. First off, which way do you clasp your bra?

2. Did reading this book change your view of a cancer diagnosis? If yes, then how?

3. Do you agree that all cancer is not created equal?

4. What do you think is more of a burden for a person, having light or medium cancer or having day-to-day chronic pain with no end in sight?

5. Do you think the same principle of lite, medium, and heavy could also be applied to veterans? Such as one veteran could have a desk job close to their hometown and others could have been in a war zone. Just a thought that like cancer survivors, not all veterans are created equal. What other situations have these variations?

6. With regards to the marriage board, do you think that was an effective tool and how could it have been improved?

7. Do you think using the "cancer card" is ethical? Why or why not?

8. Do you think God gives people cancer as part of a plan?

9. Do you think the silver lining of cancer is enough to say everything happens for a reason?

10. Did the author's perspective on blood donation encourage you in any way to start becoming a regular donor? Why or why not?

11. Do you feel the quote "I try not to say no to what the second wife will say yes to" is a realistic statement? Are there ways that you could see this applying to your own marriage or relationship? Do you think it would have a positive impact?

12. What ideas did you get from the book on how to support a friend or relative after they get a cancer diagnosis?

CPSIA information can be obtained at www.ICGtesting.com
Printed in the USA
BVOW11s0806281115

428573BV00001B/3/P